The Artistry of J. W. Remy Steins

The Artistry of J. W. Remy Steins

Lyn Ayers

Image credits:

Eric Mihan image of artwork for the University of Portland, Oregon, stein, used with permission of Andre Ammelounx, p. 22.

Image of 2.0 L Bowling Pin stein, used with permission of Les Paul, p. 115.

Image of last stein produced by J. W. Remy, used with permission of Gerd Kessler, p. 54.

J. W. Remy catalog image (title page), used with permission of Gerd Kessler, great-grandson of J. W. Remy.

J. W. Remy family photos and factory images, used with permission, pp. v, 4, 5, 6, 8, 15, 16, and 60.

Kessler family images, used with permission, pp. 10, 11, 17, and 21.

Kiln map location of vicinity of J. W. Remy and J. P. Thewalt factories, used with permission of Mrs. Hedwig Carola Bürgermeister (dec.), p. 125.

Remaining images were taken by and are the property of the author. Exceptions are noted individually.

Cover design by Jodi Tripp Photography and Graphic Design
Editing by Kari Filburn, Line by Line Copyediting

Published by Lyn Ayers
Vancouver, Washington
www.jw-remy.com

Printed in the United States of America
ISBN: 978-0-578-81017-1
Library of Congress Control Number: 2021902154

DEDICATION

To Gerd Kessler, great-grandson of J. W. Remy, who provided the primary impetus for my journey into the history of the J. W. Remy stoneware company. This book would have been impossible without his willingness to share his extensive knowledge and resources regarding the history of the company J. W. Remy.

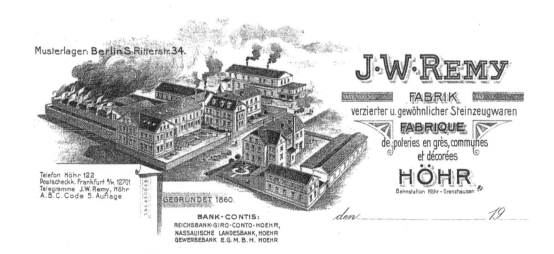

I don't imagine that there could be anyone who has published such a comprehensive insight into the world of stoneware steins. I also can't think of anybody to have assembled such a comprehensive catalog.

There are parts in your history of my family that I did not know about, which makes it even more interesting.

Thank you very much again for this very important supplement to our family history!

—*Gerd Kessler*

CONTENTS

PREFACE

During my military tour with the United States Army in Germany in 1967 and 1968, I, like many GIs, purchased beer steins as souvenirs. Upon returning home to Washington State to complete my college education, I lost interest in those souvenirs. I stored the steins on a shelf in the garage until my career stabilized in the mid-1980s. That was when I discovered Stein Collectors International (SCI) and its local chapter Pacific Stein Sammler.

At the 1993 annual SCI convention, I was impressed by the varied designs of etched J. W. Remy steins. Not surprisingly, I decided that J. W. Remy pieces would become the focus of my collection. After several years of collecting J. W. Remy, friends suggested that I had enough steins and knowledge to write a book. I didn't consider the idea seriously at the time.

As more years passed, I became increasingly intrigued with the history of the company. I began to compile information about J. W. Remy. Included was its place in Germany's Westerwald stoneware industry of the nineteenth and twentieth centuries. As I accumulated information, it became clear that this company, its history, and its products deserved to be written down and saved.

The results of what I learned about J. W. Remy are laid out for you in this book. It has three major sections. Part 1 is its history, part 2 is an overview of the artistry and variety of designs, and part 3 is a picture catalog of six hundred of the company's steins and other wares.

The purpose of this book is to introduce the breadth of artistry and quality of J. W. Remy stoneware. My hope is that you will appreciate its extensive manufacturing production as well as its design motifs.

Based on what you learn from this book, you may find an unmarked piece that you can identify as having been made by J. W. Remy.

ACKNOWLEDGMENTS

I am indebted to many friends who have provided encouragement and input through the process of writing this book.

Thanks to Master Steinologists Phil Masenheimer and Walt Vogdes for providing hours of assistance with planning and executing this book.

I especially wish to thank Les Paul for helping me recognize the artistry and attraction of J. W. Remy steins.

Steve Morris was infinitely encouraging, reminding me to keep it simple.

Professional photographer Richard Hovey donated hours of instruction on photo editing.

My sister-in-law Jan Ayers tirelessly updated photos through several photo shoots as I added steins to my collection.

My wife, Janine, devoted many hours reviewing and polishing the text. At times, she seemed more committed than I was, especially when I felt like I wasn't making progress. Her encouragement never flagged.

PART ONE

J. W. Remy Company History

CHAPTER 1

THE BEGINNING

Remy Family Background

The history of the Remy family pottery parallels the ceramics industry from the Westerwald region of Germany. During the sixteenth, seventeenth, and eighteenth centuries, most potteries were small family businesses located in the family home. Many were not registered with government authorities. The Remy family was no exception.

The Remy family can be traced to 1586, when young potter Jacques (Jakob) Remy settled in the village of Grenzhausen. Family history indicates he married a potter's widow from the nearby village of Höhr. Soon after, he moved to Höhr to manage his wife's pottery.

Family and local records indicate that Jacques Remy's son Peter Remy built a house named Schützenhof around 1650 near the center of Höhr. The land that was used for the J. W. Remy factory likely adjoined the Schützenhof property. This house still stands after 350 years as a nicely restored, half-timbered building operated as a specialty restaurant. The wooden lintel above the original front door bears the carved inscription *Peter Remi Elisabeta Uxor 1659.* According to *Die Familie Remy* [. . .] genealogical book, there are several variations in spelling of the Remy name, such as Remi, Remmy, and Remmi.

Schutzenhof

Front door lintel of the Schutzenhof

The genealogy of the Remy family is well documented. By the end of the seventeenth century, many descendants of Jacques Remy had scattered across Germany and Europe. Several had emigrated to America. Most family members continued in the pottery industry. During these early centuries, Jacques Remy and his heirs served in positions of community leadership. They had a significant role in the ceramics industry in Westerwald. Records state at least one descendant served as *Schultheis* (mayor) of Höhr. Over the centuries, the Remy name was well known and became highly respected throughout the pottery manufacturing region of Germany.

The Remy family pottery works were passed from one generation to the following, being placed in the hands of the eldest son, as was the custom of the time. Tenth-generation descendant Peter Jacob (P. J.) Remy (1800–1883) continued the family tradition as a potter. He and his family lived at Mittelstrasse 7 in Höhr. Records indicate that beginning in 1830, P. J. operated his company under the name P. J. Remy, Höhr, Thonwaaren Fabrik und Export (P. J. Remy, Höhr, Claywares Factory and Export) at that same address. The pottery specialized in white, red, black, and salt-fired claywares.

Mittelstrasse 7 ca. 1960

P. J. Remy married Katharina Gerz, "the girl next door." Her family lived across the street at Mittelstrasse 10 and also operated a pottery. P. J. and Katharina were blessed with seven children: Johann Peter Jacob, Johann Wilhelm (1833–1911), Simon Peter, Mathilde, Karl Theodore, and two other children.

Eldest son Johann Peter Jacob moved (date unknown) to Grenzhausen as a banker, leaving Johann Wilhelm (J. W.) as the oldest male remaining at home. In 1879, Simon Peter Remy, together with his sister Mathilde's husband, Anton Marzi, founded the stoneware firm Messrs. Marzi and Remy in Höhr, later moving the firm to the nearby vil-

Mittelstrasse 10 ca. 1910

lage of Grenzhausen. Karl Theodor remained a bachelor, continuing his father's pottery trading business with clay pipes and toys until his death in 1902.

J. W. Remy's Inheritance of a Pottery Factory

When Katharina's parents passed on in 1860, her inheritance, including their pottery, was transcribed to her second son, J. W. That same year, J. W. married Theresia Kuhn and assumed management of his maternal grandparent's pottery. Family records state that he founded the company in 1860 under the name J. W. Remy Fabrik und Lager (J. W. Remy Factory and Warehouse). However, it was not officially registered with the authorities until 1864. J. W. was believed to have been the first Remy to register his pottery with the government in the Nassau district.

It is not known what products the J. W. Remy firm manufactured in those beginning years. It may have been drainage pipe to keep cash flowing into the enterprise. This was probably accompanied with plain stoneware items intended primarily for food storage. Like many potteries of the area, the firm's early wares were likely hand-thrown, salt-glazed, painted, and unpainted stoneware. These were the typical gray of uncolored fired clays or they were colored with cobalt blue or manganese lavender accents. There is no mention of decorative stoneware efforts during this period.

J. W. and Theresia had five children: August, Franz, Wilhelm, Katharina, and Anna. The two older sons remained in the family pottery. Wilhelm moved to England and married into the Madame Tussaud waxworks family, although he had his own business. Katharina married Herr Kessler, and Anna married Karl Thewalt in the following years.

In order standing: Anna, Wilhelm, August, Franz, Katharina.
Seated: J. W. and Theresia
ca. 1880

By 1880, the demand for highly-decorative pottery was experiencing significant growth. This trend led to the government's establishment of the Keramische Fachschule (Ceramics Technical College) in Höhr. J. W. realized the advantages of the new design and manufacturing technologies and sent his two oldest sons, August and Franz, to the first classes at the Ceramics Technical College. He wanted his sons to learn about design and bring this knowledge to the firm.

August and Franz made significant changes in the company's operation following their technical training (ca. 1882). The emphasis on decorative style was a way to increase market appeal and thus differentiate J. W. Remy products from those of its competitors. The firm's new designs were predominantly focused on *historismus* (historical revival) motifs.

1882 class of the Höhr Ceramics Technical College
August and Franz Remy are standing
in the back row on the right

New mass-production techniques and technologies allowed the firm to expand its manufacturing output. August became the primary artist and lead modeler for the company. He consulted with Professor Alfred Kamp, an instructor at the Ceramics Technical College.

Major Expansion

Toward the end of the nineteenth century, American demand for beer steins expanded exponentially. The pottery's location straddled a main street in the center of Höhr, severely limiting J. W.'s business options. J. W. was unable to capitalize on this opportunity since he did not have available real estate to add another firing furnace.

To resolve this limitation, he forged an alliance with his daughter Anna's husband, Karl Thewalt, son of Johann Peter Thewalt, Jr. Johann Peter was the founder of the J. P. Thewalt stoneware firm located at Bergstrasse 1a, a short walking distance from the J. W. Remy factory property.

In the early 1890s, the firms completed a new round kiln on the J. P. Thewalt factory property and both shared the output. This new kiln was coal briquette-fired (not wood) using the newly developed *elfenbeinsteinzeug* (ivory stoneware) firing process. The new kiln used a lower firing temperature, which produced ivory stoneware. Major benefits of the lower firing temperature were the expanded variety of colors, unlike that of salt-glaze technology. Another significant benefit was that the firm could use the same molds for this firing process.

Company Relationships

The relationship between the J. W. Remy and J. P. Thewalt companies evolved to be more than just sharing the kiln. According to Albert Thewalt III (great-grandson of Johann Peter Thewalt, Jr.), the two companies operated as an extended family. It seems reasonable that they combined and shared aspects of business, but how this business relationship actually worked is not known.

JPT Model 1011, in catalog

JWR Model 1011, in catalog

Capacity 0.5 L

Each company retained its independence in the marketplace, including product lines and profit and loss centers. Each company had its own catalogs of wares and its own marketing and sales channels. This helps explain the rarity of duplicated designs. Family lore suggests molds were seldom traded, except in emergencies. However, Roland Henschen, in his article, "The Thewalt 'TP' Mark," stated that J. W. Remy sold molds and other technology to J. P. Thewalt.

Roland additionally wrote that family members periodically worked in each other's factory. This may account for the similar characteristics of the steins produced by both companies. For additional information about this connection, see "The Relationship between J. W. Remy and J. P. Thewalt" in the appendix.

From the 1880s to about 1895, all decoration was relief. About this time, August Remy introduced a new line of etched (incised) steins with bright color enhancements. He capitalized on these new characteristics of the ivory stoneware firing process. The etched style became a popular export to the US for both J. W. Remy and J. P. Thewalt. Both companies produced and sold relief and etched steins for several decades.

In the last years of the nineteenth century, J. W. Remy moved away from historical revival motifs. The company introduced new designs featuring popular contemporary activities, such as tavern scenes, outdoor scenes, and sports.

Exhibitions

J. W. Remy showcased its stoneware. The company was recognized at the 1888 Brussels International Exhibition and in 1889 in Kassel. According to historian Beate Dry-v. Zezschwitz, the factory took part in the 1902 Düsseldorf Industry and Trade Exhibition. In her book *Westerwälder Steinzeug des Jugendstils 1900–1914* [. . .], she wrote that the firm presented "everyday stoneware, decorated so-called Old German stoneware, and ivory stoneware."

Kassel or Brussels Exhibition
ca. 1888 or 1889

The company did not embrace *Jugendstil* (art nouveau) decorations, even though the style was becoming increasingly popular. This was probably due to August Remy's preference for the older design styles. Two Jugendstil pieces—a vase and a pitcher—are listed in the J. W. Remy *Modell Buch* (Model Book) that reference artist Albin Mueller. Neither piece has been identified. Interestingly, J. P. Thewalt did apparently purchase Jugendstil designs from Karl Görig.

The J. W. Remy firm had expanded to about sixty employees by 1904. Following this period, August Remy was becoming widely recognized for combining old decorating techniques with new designs. These designs combined early *reed-machte* (hand-scratch) decorating with colored liquid glaze paint inside the scratch lines. With this technique, designers used a sharp pointer to scratch the design into the body. This differed from the mass-production process of using a mold to produce the piece, including incising.

Family examples thrown and designed by August Remy, signed "AR," ca. 1920

The reintroduction of old techniques allowed the J. W. Remy company to participate in the Wiesbaden Exhibition of 1909. August Remy received special recognition for continuing old designs. In 1913, at the Industry and Handicraft Exhibition in Höhr, the company was again praised for retaining old designs. Following the end of the First World War, August Remy continued his design philosophy, utilizing these early manufacturing techniques until his 1928 death.

8

CHAPTER 2

THE NEXT GENERATION

Following J. W. Remy's Death

By the time of J. W.'s passing in 1911, August and Franz had assumed full factory responsibilities. With the change in ownership, the company was recognized as an *Handelsgesellschaft* (open commercial partnership). As the First World War approached, factory employment declined to between twenty and thirty employees. Demand from America for German steins was understandably disappearing. During the ensuing war, the employee count declined further to about ten workers.

Family records indicate that during the First World War, only small quantities of plain stoneware were produced. It is probable that the company discontinued its internal pewter operation during these difficult times, although there is no record of when that occurred.

Runaway inflation and high unemployment followed the armistice. Survival of either company was tenuous, while exports to America remained insignificant. After Karl Thewalt's death in 1923, the close alliance between J. P. Thewalt and J. W. Remy apparently weakened. In 1926, the Remy brothers built a new round kiln on their own property at Mittelstrasse 7. The alliance between the two companies dissolved about that time.

In 1928, disaster struck both the J. W. Remy family and firm. August and Franz, both in their sixties, caught pneumonia and died. Neither had children to inherit the business. This created a major challenge for the surviving family members. The company was undoubtedly still dealing with other issues as well. The dissolution of the J. P. Thewalt relationship, with the establishment of the new kiln, and the national financial upheaval undoubtedly all created additional difficulties.

There is little doubt that the company never fully recovered from the negative impact of this calamity.

The Kessler Era

According to custom, upon the death of an owner, the eldest son was the automatic heir. But since August and Franz had no sons, factory ownership passed to sister Katharina's eldest son, Robert Kessler. Robert, along with his two brothers, Karl and August, assumed control of operations. They had grown up in the factory and were familiar with basic operations. Robert Kessler had been away from the factory for a few years pursuing a career in ceramic products sales, thus his assumption of the sales responsibility may have been quite straightforward.

The brothers divided operational responsibilities. Robert Kessler oversaw sales and bookkeeping, his brother Karl managed production, and his other brother August took care of shipping and payroll. Richard Wittelsberger was hired in 1930 as the primary modeler. During this critical period, the Kessler brothers added a new product line of decorated fancy glazed ceramics with a utilitarian focus. This line included plates, ashtrays, bowls, and vases. The company continued to manufacture older product lines of stoneware vessels, including steins in the old ways as the market dictated.

Richard Wittelsberger
working on a punch bowl design ca. 1938

Drip-glaze tableware ca. 1937

During the military buildup prior to the Second World War, the J. W. Remy firm was required to stop producing decorative lines of products. As in the First World War, the company was permitted to manufacture only war-related utilitarian wares. All men between the ages of eighteen and fifty were conscripted into the military. That left about twenty women, children, and older men to continue factory operations.

In 1942, during the war, the old wood-fired salt-glaze kiln was finally shuttered. It was no longer economically viable to continue operation. The primary factors were a shortage of wood, the expense of salt, and the environmental restrictions due to the firing by-product of hydrochloric acid.

After the war, J. W. Remy continued its focus on utilitarian wares until the currency reform of mid-1948. The reform made additional monies available and provided the funding for the Kessler brothers to reactivate old factory molds, which had been kept in storage during the war. The firm was able to return to manufacturing beer steins using the ivory stoneware process. In 1950, the company reactivated basic pewter operations by hiring Richard Wittelsberger's father as department manager. Business picked up again, probably due to a demand by tourists and American soldiers for souvenirs of their time in Germany.

Robert Kessler at his desk
ca. 1970

During the ensuing years, business levels continued to improve. Employment expanded to around thirty-five employees. However, the firm's factory location in the city center continued to be an issue. Its buildings straddled Mittelstrasse, an increasingly busy arterial street. The J. W. Remy firm presumably came under increasing pressure from the city to move.

Unfortunately, sales and profits during the late 1940s and the 1950s did not justify a factory relocation nor were they adequate to secure a financial future for the next generation of Kesslers. Realizing this, the Kessler children pursued professions outside the pottery industry. The words of Gerd Kessler drive this point home.

I was no exception. I went into engineering and left home for Canada about 1954, although I grew up in the factory doing a myriad of odd jobs. I believe I must have attended every firing of the kilns from about age six or seven until I moved to Canada. I vividly recall at the age of five or six racing around the kiln making sure the vents were properly adjusted during the firings. I was not any good at working with clay, nor was I encouraged to develop those skills.

11

End of an Era

In 1959, Karl Kessler died, followed by the death of brother August Kessler in 1965. Unable to continue the operation by himself, Robert Kessler, in poor health as well, shut down the firm in 1966. The stoneware firms of Gilles u. Sohn and Werner Corzelius acquired equipment and molds. S. P. Gerz purchased a large number of molds.

Prior to the closure, Robert Kessler ensured that all employees were successfully employed by other potteries in the area. Having been with the firm some thirty years as the primary artist, Richard Wittelsberger was employed by Gilles u. Sohn.

As a matter of family pride, there were no outstanding debts or unmet commitments when the company ceased operations. The factory buildings were eventually demolished to accommodate street expansion.

Following 102 years of operation, the stoneware firm of J. W. Remy came to an end. After nearly four centuries of involvement with the Westerwald pottery industry, this line of direct Jacques Remy descendants had now been separated from the pottery industry. However, there are many cousins from other lines of the Remy family who are still associated with the ceramics industry.

A closing note: The *Westerwaldkreis* (Westerwald District) recently recognized several of the early major contributors to the pottery heritage of the region by naming city streets after them. Notably, there is now a Jacques Remy Strasse (street) in Höhr-Grenzhausen.

PART TWO

J. W. Remy Product Line

CHAPTER 3

PRODUCT OVERVIEW

For more than a century, the J. W. Remy firm produced a broad variety of ceramic products for use in the home. An extensive line of beer steins were made in relief and etched styles. Decorations and motifs were often modified and re-used for multiple items, and adapted to reflect changing public tastes. Jugendstil design characteristics were incorporated beginning around 1900.

The J. W. Remy Model Book, factory catalogs, and sales history are the three primary sources of information about their products.

The J. W. Remy Model Book

The handwritten Model Book was the company's master journal. Entries include model number, capacity or height, price, and a brief description of each piece. It presents an impressive record of the breadth of J. W. Remy's product offerings.

The book consists of three sections. The first section covers model numbers 50 through 1793, and the third section, likely created following the Second World War, resumes with model number 1794 and continues to model 1960, although many numbers in this section are empty, presumably never assigned.

Page from the Model Book
ca. 1900

The second section, likely initiated following the death of the Remy brothers in 1928, deals only with kitchen tableware. Model numbers range from 3001 to 3814, including the newly developed crackle-type flow glaze wares. A few examples of these items were pictured previously in The Kessler Era section of chapter 2. None have been seen in the United States.

Taken together, sections 1 and 2 list some 1,700 forms numbered from 50 to 1960. About 1,275 different pieces are steins or related items, including pokals, punch bowls, vases, or plaques.

As a means of extending their offerings, steins were often produced with a choice of flat or recessed base. The recessed base made the stein visually taller and more appealing, while also fetching a higher price. Such examples have separate entries and different model numbers in the Model Book.

Many of the model numbers above about 1400 seem to be for custom designs and special orders. One example is model 1451, in which the description includes a cryptic reference to *Gi*. This is immediately followed by more than one hundred models containing the same notation. Other examples from around the same time include the letters *Fd* or *Fol*, *Gerh*, *Kru*, and *Mih*. There is corroborating evidence indicating that *Mih* refers to steins produced in the 1950s for American wholesaler Eric Mihan. About thirty-five entries in the Model Book bear the *Mih* designation. Gerd Kessler speculated that the other marks may represent orders placed by small local potteries that did not have their own kilns—*Gi* for Gilles u. Sohn, *Gerh* for Gerharz, and *Kru* for Krumeich. *Fd* might refer to the firm of Johann Josef Ferdinand.

Page from the Model Book showing likely custom orders for colleges ca. 1950

Steins produced as commemoratives or souvenirs for the US market are rarely listed in the Model Book, and, while several examples are known to bear the JWR logo, few have impressed model numbers.

While the JWR Model Book provides considerable information about their offerings, there remain some challenges. The descriptions it provides are handwritten in Old German script and many employ cryptic notations. In addition, many of the terms used are no longer familiar to today's German readers.

A larger disappointment is the fact that dates appear only as infrequent notations. Items are listed in order by model number, but some model numbers are left blank, apparently to accommodate later entries. As a result, although entries are generally listed in chronological order, and it appears that the second section was created post-World War I, the Model Book is not reliable for specific dating purposes.

Unfortunately, no equivalent to the JWR Model Book has surfaced for the Thewalt firm.

Catalogs

J. W. Remy catalogs exist from several different time periods. In total, they depict nearly 1,100 items. One catalog of about three hundred pieces shows a ratio of steins to non-steins of about 2:1. Catalogs depicting models numbered above 1375 are rare. One later catalog shows a few steins with music box bases with model numbers in the range of 1650 to 1820.

Only one J. P. Thewalt catalog is known. It pictures nearly one hundred relief steins with model numbers between 1000 and 1213.

Contemporary steins
ca. 1900–1914

Catalog page of historical revival (historismus) ewers and vases ca. 1880–1900

Auctions and Online Sales

Several thousand pieces attributed to either J. W. Remy or J. P. Thewalt can be found in auction catalogs. Many more pieces bearing the characteristics of these firms have appeared, but not attributed to a factory. Additionally, many pieces from both firms have been sold online. While photographs of these items can help to determine model numbers or even to identify particular examples, they also provide indication of how common or rare an individual piece may be.

Five-Digit Model Numbers

An unexplained curiosity is presented by J. W. Remy steins that bear a five-digit model number. In all cases, the leading digit is a *1*. As noted earlier, no steins are listed in the Model Book—or available catalogs—with numbers higher than 1960. In fact, if the first digit is ignored, steins bearing a five-digit model number may be found in the Model Book and catalogs using the last four digits alone. For example, the model marked 11046 is identified in the Model Book as 1046.

The reason for this additional digit is not known, although there is a possible—and reasonable—explanation. As mentioned earlier, the J. P. Thewalt firm had a cooperative relationship with J. W. Remy. For several decades, both companies produced similar steins, and the model numbers for the two firms overlap in the range of about 1000 to the middle 1600s. Since steins from both firms were fired in the same kiln, the most likely explanation for this extra digit was to distinguish J. W. Remy's steins from those of J. P. Thewalt.

Five-digit 11046
base mark

Only one example is known with a five-digit model number and a J. P. Thewalt logo. However, that stein is not depicted in the J. P. Thewalt catalog with that number. The most probable explanation for this is that a JWR stein was mistaken for a JPT stein before sending to the kiln, and the JPT logo was added in error.

Four-digit 1046
catalog number

CHAPTER 4

ARTWORK AND DECORATION

Early Years

Little documentation exists regarding the first twenty years of the J. W. Remy company. It is probable that production during those years consisted primarily of utilitarian hand-thrown pieces. The drainage pipe product line, which was believed to have been inherited from the Gerz in-laws, was surely continued.

After completing their studies at the Ceramics Technical College in 1882, August and Franz were integrated into the company's operations. August Remy was aggressive in leading the decorative efforts of his father's company, and, with Franz, the company quickly adopted historismus (historical revival) designs. This was important for the company's competitive position in the market since other potteries were adopting their own versions of historical revival designs.

Another benefit of August and Franz's training is that they were able to introduce the use of plaster molds into the manufacturing process. This advancement enabled machine production of multiple copies of identical pieces. The technology resulted in lower costs and higher production volumes.

During this early period, the pieces were fired in the salt-glaze kiln using primarily cobalt blue enhancements.

147 5.0 L

Expanded Operations and Designs

The alliance of J. W. Remy and J. P. Thewalt and the construction of a new kiln in the early 1890s resulted in a major expansion of operations. Not only was firing capacity increased, but replacing wood with coal briquettes enabled better temperature control, less firing loss, and better quality.

The lower firing temperatures of the new kiln not only enabled a new elfenbein-steinzeug (ivory stoneware) line, but it also brought about

1016 0.5 L   791 0.5 L

the use of bright multicolor glazes, not previously possible. Molds that had been used for salt-glazed items now were able to be used for polychrome and ivory stoneware as well.

In the early 1900s, demand for modern and Jugendstil (art nouveau) style designs replaced historical revival decorations. Historian Beate Dry-v. Zezschwitz wrote that around 1903 or 1904, J. W. Remy purchased several Jugendstil designs from artist Karl Görig. A half-dozen Jugendstil designs that have similarities to Görig designs are pictured in the catalogs, but without any reference to Görig. However, as stated previously, August Remy was apparently resistant to art nouveau style. There is little evidence of additional activity in this direction after his father's death in 1911.

Artistic design evolved to what was being referred to as *contemporary*. Modern themes focused on German life of the time. Scenes of taverns, drinking, outdoor, hiking, and sports were popular. Designs also included themes based on paintings by popular artists of the period, such as Franz von DeFregger, Heinrich Schlitt, and Eduard von Gruetzner. August embraced this contemporary style and incorporated those design elements into many of the company's wares.

Somewhat in parallel with this movement, artistic styles began to focus on etched (incised) steins intended primarily for the American market.

August Remy's Hand-Thrown, Hand-Decorated Line

August had a strong personal liking for the hand-thrown and hand-scratched (reetmachte) pieces from the early 1800s. After the end of the First World War, he indulged this interest by designing a new line of steins and containers in this older style. Pieces in this line were fired in the salt-glaze kiln using cobalt blue and manganese lavender glaze.

Production of these items was labor intensive and required skills that were fast disappearing from industrialized factories, both factors that constrained production. Examples from this line are scarce and rarely found outside Germany.

All known examples bear the company logo with no model number. There are no listings in the Model Book for any items from this line. Each piece was hand-thrown and hand-decorated, with the result that each was unique.

Family members understand that August threw and decorated many pieces with his own hands. This was highly unusual for a master potter in an executive position. Several examples signed with the initials AR on the base are held in Kessler family collections. I feel very fortunate to have four pieces with logos from this line in my collection, although none have his initials.

Two pieces on right signed by August Remy ca. 1920
Flask on left decorated by Gerd Kessler's daughter Susanne ca. 1984
Used with permission of the Kessler family

By August Remy 2.0 L
ca. 1920

Era of the Kessler Brothers

Following the deaths of August and Franz in 1928, the Kessler brothers introduced a line of decorative tableware with fancy drip glazes (see drip-glaze tableware image on p. 10). Family photos depict other decorative pieces of the art styles of the 1940s. Production of this line may have been discontinued around 1948. Examples have not been identified in the United States.

1864 0.5 L
University of Portland
designed by Eric Mihan

Copy of original Eric Mihan artwork ca. 1950
for University of Portland submitted to J. W. Remy
Used with permission of Andre Ammelounx

After the Second World War, souvenir sales to American occupying forces and tourists began to increase. One example was Eric Mihan's college souvenir designs. During the early 1950s, his steins were manufactured by J. W. Remy as well as other potteries. These steins have only Mihan's copyright information on the base and no other identifying model numbers or logos. However, the Model Book does include assigned numbers for those special-order Mihan steins, which likely indicates additional production orders.

During the two decades following the German 1948 financial reset, the company continued to produce steins for domestic use, the tourist market, and custom orders from other smaller potteries. These pieces often have no incised model numbers, though a logo can occasionally be found on pieces likely sold at retail by J. W. Remy.

CHAPTER 5

CLASSICAL ETCHED STEINS

The J. W. Remy stoneware firm is primarily known for its etched (incised) steins. Their distinctive characteristics make them quite easy to identify.

Etched steins use incised black lines to separate areas of different color or to provide detail. The flat surface of the body image has a matte finish, and with rare exception, scenes on etched steins are in full color and wrap most of the body. Interiors are glazed white. The top and base rims are usually a high-glaze chocolate or caramel color. Body bands above and below the central scene are highly glazed, often in a soft pink or lavender color. The same color is often found on the high-gloss handle as well. Molded handles were produced in a limited number of designs, and they are also a useful identifier (see chapter 12). Glaze skips on the handles are common and should not be interpreted as wear or damage.

717 1.0 L

Etched steins are often fitted with etched ceramic inlaid lids. The central design of these inlays is matte finished like the body design and usually encircled with a ring of high-glazed beads. An undecorated outer rim in a caramel color usually completes the inlay.

Approximately 160 different models of J. W. Remy and J. P. Thewalt etched steins are known. Only about 10 percent are marked with one of their logos. Dates handwritten on several J. W. Remy catalog pages indicate etched steins were made between 1895 and 1914. Capacities range from 0.125 liters (L) to 5.0 L, with the vast majority being in the middle sizes.

884 0.5 L

Stein manufacturers S. P. Gerz, A. J. Thewalt, and M. Girmscheid made a few etched steins with one or two attributes similar to those of J. W. Remy/J. P. Thewalt steins. However, the predominant characteristics of steins produced by these companies are substantially different from the attributes of pieces from the Remy-Thewalt alliance. Even so, these other examples have often been attributed to J. W. Remy. A typical example is the beading on some S. P. Gerz inlays, where the beads look like links in a chain, while other lid characteristics are similar to lids from the alliance.

Highly Decorated Etched Steins

Instead of the simple relief body bands typically used for etched steins, a subset of about twenty models utilize wide relief bands above and below the central scene. These bands wrap around the body and display design elements that complement the central motif. They are often in a brighter glaze than the typical Remy-Thewalt alliance etched steins. The high-glaze figural inlaid lids on these steins also complement the theme or motif of the stein. They rarely have the characteristic beading or the caramel-colored glazed rim of etched inlays. Capacities of this group range from 0.25 L to 2.5 L.

Themes of many steins in this group include popular activities of the time, such as hunting, bicycling, bowling, or 4-F gymnastics.

1046 1.5 L   958 0.25 L   1434 0.3 L   11070 1.0 L

Additionally, there are several groups or sets of steins within this category. Examples are the Renaissance scenes (1046 or 11070) and the Dutch scenes (11072). For more information on these sets, see chapter 10, "Sets and Series."

Etched and Relief Steins

There are approximately twenty-five stein models that combine etched and relief decorative techniques. In this small but noteworthy group, the matte backgrounds of the scenes are typical of etched steins, but the foregrounds are executed in relief. The remaining design elements of these steins are typical of etched steins. Steins in this group are found in sizes ranging from 0.25 L up to at least 1.5 L.

Whether these steins were produced by J. W. Remy or J. P. Thewalt is uncertain. None of them appear in either J. W. Remy or J. P. Thewalt catalogs. A few examples with three-digit model numbers are marked with the *JWR* trademark. Most, however, have model numbers in the range between 1300 and 1399, suggesting they were produced by J. P. Thewalt. None of the pieces found to date bear the *JPT* logo.

1453 0.5 L   11072 0.5 L

1358 1.0 L

1356 0.5 L with handle

1352 1.5 L

1351 1.0 L

CHAPTER 6

RELIEF STEINS

The vast majority of products manufactured by the J. W. Remy firm were executed in molded relief, even though the company is primarily known for its full-color ivory etched steins.

The company produced salt-glazed wares continuously from the 1860s until 1942 when the salt-glaze kiln was deactivated. Pieces from the first twenty years of operation are rare and have not been identified in the US. Items from that period would have been hand thrown, and, if decorated, would have been either glazed or, later, hand incised. The primary coloring agent in use at the time was cobalt blue due to cost. Cobalt remained the dominant color throughout the lifetime of the salt-glaze kiln, although an occasional stein can be found with manganese lavender highlights.

With the completion of the new kiln around

247 1.75 L

135 2.75 L

748 0.5 L

687 0.5 L

673 1.5 L

1890, the J. W. Remy and J. P. Thewalt firms were able to produce steins in any of three ways: cobalt blue salt glaze, two-color ivory, or full-color ivory. Also, by this point in time, molds had replaced hand-thrown pieces. In fact, as shown here, a single mold could be used to produce the same item in three finishes.

752 0.5 L

Full-color ivory   Salt glaze   Two-color ivory

The sharpness of relief detail varied widely. When comparing salt-glazed with ivory relief examples of the same form, the salt-glazing generally shows finer detail. The ivory process required dipping the piece in a liquid-glass sealer prior to firing, a step not needed for salt-glazing. Unfortunately, the sealer often masked some of the fine detail of the design.

The quality of the relief detail from J. W. Remy was at its finest in the late 1800s. Many of its pieces had superlative detail in quality of the clays, in design, and in glazing. Over the following decades, the industry matured. Stoneware pieces became more of a commodity as the market became more competitive. Production quality was constrained by the military buildup prior to the First World War. Stoneware produced between the world wars was more utilitarian with fewer decorative design elements. After the Second World War, the overall quality suffered greatly, as both manufacturing costs and competition increased.

J. W. Remy catalogs show the evolution of designs over time from historical revival to modern to art nouveau (Jugendstil). Obviously, all pieces were made of ivory stoneware after deactivation of the old wood-fired salt-glaze kiln.

The modelers for relief steins created miscellaneous themes and sets similar to those found with etched steins. Several of these additional groupings are addressed in chapter 10.

Outdoor Relief Steins

This subgroup of nearly twenty examples from J. W. Remy consists of heavy-relief steins without the common decorative top band. Instead, the band was replaced with sky since all designs are outdoor scenes. Full-color steins in this group have a light-blue sky in matte finish. Occasionally, examples are found in blue-gray salt glaze or two-color ivory, although most are full color. The relief and glaze details are a better quality than mainstream color relief pieces from the company. Most steins larger than 1.0 L have high-quality poured pewter lids. Smaller examples have either inlaid ceramic insert lids or conical spun-pewter lids. Sizes range from 0.3 L to 3.0 L.

The themes of these steins are lighthearted and often show comical situations or have humorous touches. Examples include scenes of outdoor revelry, finger-twisting contests, singing, and typical Bavarian-style rocking to the music. Moons have smiling faces, and flying birds and butterflies are often included to add warmth to the scene.

938 2.0 L

777 2.0 L

966 1.5 L

Vine-Accented Steins

J. W. Remy produced another family of heavy-relief steins with vine-accent decorations. Instead of typical bands, these artistic bands emulate twisted vines embellished with green berries. The vines are usually located just below the top rim and just above the base. The body decoration is enclosed between them. The handles emulate a twisted vine. These are usually referred to as twisted-vine handles.

11228 (2.0 L) showing the handle and the front   1110 (0.5 L) showing the handle and the front

The majority of steins in this group have a saying in German lettering that wraps the base. The saying is printed in ivory letters with a dark-brown background. The body scenes have images of people from different time periods, from the Renaissance to the nineteenth century.

The model number for this subgroup is usually found near the lower handle attachment, beneath the handle, or embedded in the body's design. Typically, other steins have the model number incised on the base.

Sometimes the model number is difficult to decipher due to thick glaze that fills the incised digits. The handle attachment occasionally hides part of the number, adding to the difficulty. However, many steins in the group can be identified with a little research since most are pictured in J. W. Remy catalogs.

Capacities range from 0.5 L to several liters. These were probably made

11074 0.5 L

shortly after the First World War into the difficult times leading up to the Second World War. Some examples lack a capacity mark; most are not marked to indicate country of origin, indicating they were probably not intended for export. This is undoubtedly due to the antipathy in foreign lands toward German-manufactured items of this period.

Full-color 0.5 L and 1.0 L steins generally have pewter lids, while the two-color ivory stoneware examples nearly always have a figural two-color ceramic inlay. The full-color steins required more handwork, and the pewter was more expensive than the ceramic

11238 0.5 L

inlay, making these steins more expensive to purchase. The company traditionally mounted more expensive lids on steins that had a higher manufacturing cost; the opposite was also true.

Based upon the number of pieces presently known, sixty to seventy-five steins with vine characteristics were likely made.

No example of a salt-glaze fired piece has been seen in this group. Notable is that most vine-accented steins are marked with a five-digit model number.

Only two examples of the vine-theme steins have been seen with a manufacturer's logo. The first, model 11065, has an impressed *JWR* base mark; the second, model 11045, is marked *JPT*. This is the only five-digit model directly connected to J. P. Thewalt.

At least four companies produced steins with twisted-vine handles. In the absence of a company logo on the base, J. W. Remy's vine-accented steins may be confused with relief steins from one of these other manufacturers. Although there are noticeable differences with handles on relief steins made by M. Girmscheid and A. J. Thewalt, the twisted-vine handles on Eckhart and Engler are virtually identical on their 1.0 L and larger steins.

Example of five-digit marking vs. original four-digit
11111/1111 0.5 L

CHAPTER 7

CHARACTER STEINS

J. W. Remy produced approximately thirty different character steins. Most were fired as ivory stoneware decorated with either two-color or full-color. Rare examples in blue-gray salt glaze have been seen. Nearly half represent an animal with a rotund body. Each has a banner showing a German phrase across the front of the body. Many of the animal steins incorporate the tail into the design of the handle. This odd-shaped handle often interferes with the pewter strap attaching the lid. As a result, it is common to find an animal character stein with a damaged or repaired strap.

Munich Child 900 1.0 L
Two-color

Munich Child 901 0.5 L
Full-color

Gentleman Dog
768 0.5 L Full-color

Another variation includes the Munich Child, the only design made in three sizes: 1.0 L, 0.5 L, and 0.25 L. The Bowling Pin stein was made in two sizes: 0.5 L and a master 2.0 L. There are two different capacities each for the rare miniature Cat stein and Rabbit stein: 0.25 and 0.125 L.

Character stein model numbers are usually three digits or four digits, although there are a few five-digit versions. Those with three-digit model numbers were likely produced around the turn of the twentieth century prior to the First World War. The lids on the three-digit pieces usually have a pewter rim with a ceramic figural insert completing the head or upper body of the character. Early pieces appear to be of a more classical depiction by representing either people or animals.

Steins with either four or five digits in their model numbers were likely designed later. Their lids have less pewter. In place of a pewter rim, there is only a strap, tang, and a 0.25-inch pewter plug that attaches the pottery lid to the stein. It is probable these steins date between the two world wars. Character steins in this grouping include buildings and towers.

There are several character steins from J. W. Remy that have not been seen. The Gentleman Rooster (974) appears in only one catalog, although it is listed in the Model Book. The 0.5 L Woman Tavern Owner (973) and the 0.125 L Rabbit (787) are in the Model Book as well, although neither is pictured in any catalog. They either never went into production or were produced in a small quantity, possibly due to manufacturing complications or little demand.

During the late 1960s, the stoneware firm of M. Girmscheid introduced several character steins based on J. W. Remy models. To minimize confusion, M. Girmscheid marked its versions with different model numbers. Additional differences include brighter glaze colors.

Gentleman Cat
767 0.5 L
Full-color ivory

Bowling Ball
1236 0.5 L
Jugendstil elements, no pewter rim
Two-color ivory

Gentleman Boch
972 0.5 L
Two-color ivory

CHAPTER 8

COMMEMORATIVE AND SOUVENIR STEINS

Lewis and Clark
Exposition 0.5 L

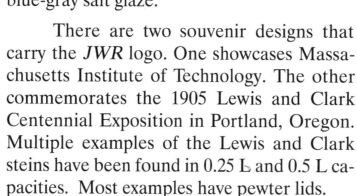

Lewis and Clark
Exposition 0.25 L

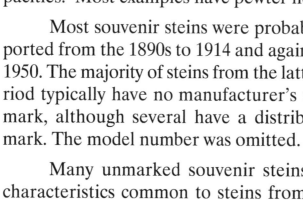

Milwaukee
0.5 L

J. W. Remy made and supplied a number of special designs for the American market. The Washington, DC set of four unnumbered etched steins highlight famous buildings in Washington, DC. They were obviously intended as tourist souvenir pieces.

The majority of J. W. Remy souvenir steins are relief, and they can be found in a variety of firing or decorating variations. They appear as two-color ivory, full-color ivory, or blue-gray salt glaze.

There are two souvenir designs that carry the *JWR* logo. One showcases Massachusetts Institute of Technology. The other commemorates the 1905 Lewis and Clark Centennial Exposition in Portland, Oregon. Multiple examples of the Lewis and Clark steins have been found in 0.25 L and 0.5 L capacities. Most examples have pewter lids.

Most souvenir steins were probably exported from the 1890s to 1914 and again after 1950. The majority of steins from the latter period typically have no manufacturer's trademark, although several have a distributor's mark. The model number was omitted.

Many unmarked souvenir steins have characteristics common to steins from J. W. Remy. Glaze treatments, handles, and capacity marks all support a theory that they were made by this company. Examples include steins made for the 1904 St. Louis Exposition in Mis-

Etched Washington, DC
0.5 L

FOE
Fraternal Order
of Eagles
0.5 L

souri. There are several examples of salt-glazed souvenir steins for different cities in the Midwest.

Commemorative steins were made that celebrated different social organizations, such as the Independent Order of Odd Fellows, Loyal Order of Moose, and other contemporaries. The Freemasons ordered an etched design. It has a J. W. Remy model number (1180) and is described in the Model Book. Similar to the custom-designed Freemasons stein, several commemoratives were modified from J. W. Remy standard production designs. Examples are the pictured steins, modified for the Benevolent and Protective Order of Elks (BPOE).

11108 with BPOE
modifications 0.5 L

11127 with BPOE
modifications 2.0 L

In the early 1950s, German entrepreneur Eric Mihan designed a large group of college-specific steins for the American market. Every piece has the date and the phrase "Copyright Eric Mihan" either incised or ink stamped onto the base. None include a manufacturer's name. According to auctioneer Andre Ammelounx, Eric Mihan provided steins for more than one-hundred American colleges and universities. These steins have various scenes of interest at the different schools. These usually include the school mascot and important campus buildings, as well as the school insignia. Mihan supplied the college bookstores that sold the steins to students to commemorate their university years. As he received orders, he placed orders with German beer stein factories. J. W. Remy provided some thirty models, since the Model Book apparently documents a relationship with Eric Mihan. Examples of original design paperwork for these custom pieces have been found. The design paperwork for the University of Portland is shown at the end of chapter 4, used with permission of Andre Ammelounx.

CHAPTER 9

NON-STEIN WARES

Early vase ca. 1890
141 10" Tall

Vase ca. 1890 ivory
stoneware 321 10" Tall

Although wares other than steins are rarely found in the American marketplace, the J. W. Remy catalogs and Model Book list a significant number of non-stein pieces. In the early years, catalogs show many punch bowls, vases, and tobacco-related items. Various catalogs indicate that up to 40 percent of what J. W. Remy produced were not steins. In the 1950s and 1960s, the company shifted away from steins to primarily designing punch bowls.

Of the two hundred pieces pictured in the J. P. Thewalt catalog, fifty are not steins, and of that fifty, half are small stoneware figurines.

Punch bowl ca. 1880
143 8.0 L

Tobacco jar ca. 1880
331 1.0 Kg

Punch bowl ca. 1890
159 4.5 L

Drinking horn
11130 2.0 L

Plaque ca. 1885
839 10.5" in diameter

CHAPTER 10

SETS AND SERIES

Stein collectors inevitably find it necessary to organize and define their collections in some way, whether it's by manufacturer, material, size, theme, artist, designer, age, style, or something else. Thus, a collector may seek 0.5 L relief steins featuring the Munich Child, or miniatures, or souvenir steins. J. W. Remy offers several groupings that spark collecting appeal because these steins obviously belong together.

The four etched Student steins produced by the alliance between J. W. Remy and J. P. Thewalt depict the usual four American high school or college class levels (see below). The steins are shown in order by model number, left to right. Noting that the normal progression of classes is Freshy, Soph, Junior, and Senior, the Junior stein seems to be out of the expected model number order. Ron Gray has hypothesized that the German designer may not have been that familiar with the American education system and incorrectly positioned the Junior stein as the first of the sequence.

Junior
1393 0.5 L

Freshy
1394 0.5 L

Soph
1395 0.5 L

Senior
1396 0.5 L

Oftentimes, highly popular models were made in more than one size. The Surprised Knight is a prime example since it was made in three sizes, 0.25 L, 0.5 L, and 1.5 L (two of which are shown below). The change in size necessitated changes to the overall body design.

Another example of the same design appearing on two or more different models is the group of Seated Troubadour steins (see below). Two of these, 564 and 612, are both 1.0 L in size, but one has a flat base and the other a recessed base, making that stein taller.

954 0.5 L   958 0.25 L   564 1.0 L   612 1.0 L   498 2.0 L

The Surprised Knight   The Seated Troubadour

The Washington, DC set featuring famous buildings that was mentioned in chapter 8 is notable. All of the steins in the set are uncommon, with the Washington Monument stein being seen only once. The ceramic lids have no pewter ring, so they close directly against the ceramic rim. This often causes damage to either the lid or the rim, possibly explaining why many of these steins are found without lids.

J. W. Remy often used various putti or winged cherubs inside a cartouche as the focus element on a variety of pieces, offering another affinity group for collectors. This style grew out of the influence of the historical revival period, likely indicating pre-1900 design. These decorations appear on relief steins in either salt-glazed or two-color ivory stoneware. The motif can be found on 0.5 L to 3.0 L steins as well as tobacco jars.

The five-piece etched Farming set is an impressive J. W. Remy series. Each piece depicts different aspects of a crop harvest. The model numbers are in sequence, indicating they were likely designed at the same time. The 5.0 L model is the largest etched stein made by J. W. Remy.

721 5.0 L   724 4.0 L   722 3.0 L   725 2.0 L   723 1.5 L

The Medieval and the Dutch series are excellent examples of a highly decorated etched group. The main decoration and the top and bottom body bands, which reflect the primary theme, wrap around the entire stein.

11095 2.0 L   11094 1.5 L   11098 1.0 L   11072 0.5 L   11079 0.25 L

Another notable group is the set of relief steins named Good Times. Made in several different sizes, they all feature the same scene of friends sitting at a table spending an enjoyable afternoon together. Normally found in full-color relief, at least one model (773) was also made in blue-gray salt glaze. The J. W. Remy catalog also features a seven-piece service consisting of the 3.0 L master and six 0.25 L steins (773).

791 0.5 L

942 0.5 L

773 0.25 L

729 3.0 L

773 0.25 L

CHAPTER 11

PANORAMAS

722 3.0 L

Unlike most of its competitors, J. W. Remy designed many of its steins with scenes that wrapped the entire body. Incorporating this design element into its steins increased the pictorial interest in its pieces. However, it can be challenging to capture the full artistry, even while holding and rotating the stein in an attempt to view the entire scene.

Digital photo-editing software offers the ability to stitch multiple images together. Although time-consuming, the resulting panorama—a view of the scene in its entirety—brings out the full artistry and impact of what the artist wanted to share.

Several examples follow. The variation in color between the steins and the panoramas is due to different lighting conditions.

1094 1.5 L

961 2.0 L

855 1.0 L

11166 2.0 L

43

1397 1.5 L

1388 1.5 L

44

CHAPTER 12

IDENTIFICATION CHARACTERISTICS

Handles

When drinking vessels were hand thrown, handles were simply clay rolled by hand into a C-shaped loop. The advent of molds in the latter half of the nineteenth century enabled handles to be decorated without additional labor, and reproducible handles came to be viewed as part of the overall stein design.

Since molds for handles were made by many firms for their own use, handles became an added means of identification of unmarked pieces.

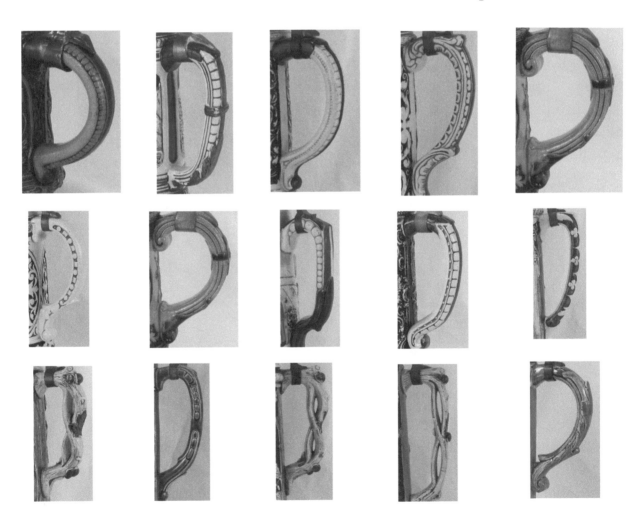

Like many of its competitors, J. W. Remy designed its own molds for its handles. Following the completion of schooling of August and Franz, the company focused on historical revival motifs, including the creation of adding a unique handle for each stein. Over the years, the industry matured, competition increased, and the firm evolved to designing handles that could be interchanged on multiple steins. As previously stated, handles are also a helpful indicator when identifying a J. W. Remy stein.

Pictured on the previous page are handles from ca. 1885 through the First World War when most steins from J. W. Remy used one of these fairly common handles.

Lids

Pewter Lids

At various times, both J. W. Remy and J. P. Thewalt companies had their own pewter operations. According to surviving documents, J. W. Remy poured and mounted pewter lids in-house for much of the company's existence. Prior to the buildup leading to the First World War, the cost of pewter was not a significant portion of the final cost of the completed piece. High-quality pewter lids are usually found on earlier blue-gray relief salt-glazed steins. Occasionally, a higher-quality, larger ivory stoneware stein will be seen with a poured lid.

It is probable that J. W. Remy's master molds for pewter work, lacking any specific identification characteristics, were purchased from mold manufacturers. The same basic designs were likely purchased and used by other potteries. As a result, using a pewter lid or thumb-lift design as an identification tool is not very useful.

Examples of poured lids   A typical spun lid

Over the years, the cost of pewter increased substantially. J. W. Remy responded by reducing the amount of pewter in its lids. Instead of pouring lids, which required more pewter, they "spun" or pressed sheets of thin pewter into shape, thereby reducing the cost.

The development of inlaid lids was another response to the increasing cost of pewter. Inlaid lids involved replacing the pyramidal center of the lid with a piece of ceramic inserted into the outer pewter ring. The ceramic was usually either etched or relief to match the type of stein. Worthy of note is that inlaid lids are rarely found on salt-glazed steins.

Etched Inlaid Lids

J. W. Remy developed many different designs of etched inlaid lids. Usually the design in the center of the inlay has the same matte finish as the body. The high-glazed outer rim also has the characteristic caramel-brown glaze typical of J. W. Remy steins. Nearly all of its etched inlays have a ring of beading around the inlay.

Examples of various etched inlaid lids
from both J. W. Remy and J. P. Thewalt

1393   1394   1395   1396

With only one known exception, inlay design was entirely independent of the stein upon which it was mounted. The exception? The Student set (Freshy, Soph, Junior, and Senior), where each stein had its own unique inlay.

The impact of the war and the following reparations dramatically increased the cost of pewter. In response, J. W. Remy transitioned to a few very low-cost lids using less pewter, similar to the Washington, DC lids discussed in chapter 10.

Relief Inlaid Lids

J. W. Remy relief inlays are similar in style to etched inlays. However, they don't have beading or a caramel glaze ring. These inlays are usually in the same colors as the body of the stein. As with etched inlays, they rarely reflect the theme of the body. Similar relief inlays are uncommon on other manufacturers' steins.

Examples of relief inlaid lids

48

Figural Inlaid Lids

Figural inlays fall into two general classifications. One is a representation of a standing person. This inlay is found on many larger etched pieces. These figures can also be found on vine motif relief steins. A two-color ivory stein will have a figural inlay in the same body colors, whereas a full-color stein will usually have a pewter lid.

The second classification of figural inlays is where the lid is an extension of the theme of the stein. Rather than representing a person, it reinforces the theme of the stein with a physical form. For example, a stein with an outdoor theme might have a figural lid inlay of a mountain peak. These are mostly found on steins from the category of etched with high-glaze relief decoration.

Examples of figural inlaid lids

Marks

Steins from J. W. Remy can often be identified by the markings on the piece, to include logos, base marks, capacity marks, and model numbers. J. W. Remy steins may have marks in all, a few, or none of the following locations: on the base or near the top rim, incised within the scene, on the back, or underneath the handle.

Base marks consist of one or more of the following: a logo, a model number, the word *Germany*, the capacity, and one or two quality-control characters.

49

Logo Marks

Most J. W. Remy steins are not marked with a manufacturer's logo. However, if one does have a logo, it is usually found on the base. Several exceptions include milk jugs. For an unknown reason, these typically have the logo incised on the back, below the handle's lower attachment.

Logo with periods pre-1918   Logo with no periods pre-1918

The most common logo is a corner-cut rectangle framing the letters *J.W.R.* This design was used until some time around the First World War. A smaller variation containing the letters *JWR* (sans periods) is generally found on steins smaller than 0.5 L.

Various logos over the years

A logo that is believed to have been introduced soon after the First World War, but prior to 1934, is an incised oval ring containing the name *J.W. Remy* on the upper side and *Hoehr* (English spelling) along the bottom. A similar version has *J.W. REMY* incised in an arc above *Höhr*. Usage dates are not known for these marks, but both versions have been seen on steins probably dating from the same time period.

Shortly after the Second World War, the company adopted a completely different logo. This new logo consists of the conjoined letters *JWR*. The center of the *W* extends above the other two letters and is topped with the image of a tiny stein. It can be found either incised or ink stamped.

J. P. Thewalt logos

The logo for J. P. Thewalt is formed from the conjoined letters *J, P,* and *T.* The downstroke of the *T* (for Thewalt) also serves as the downstroke of the *P* (Peter), and a dot above the downstroke completes the otherwise absent *J* (Johann). At the time, the *J* was often represented as a lowercase letter *i.*

There are two versions of the J. P. Thewalt logo: one with a period, or dot, and one without. The reason for the difference is not known.

Base Marks

The base on most J. W. Remy steins manufactured in the ivory process is either flat or recessed. Flat bases are typically not glazed. Recessed bases are almost always glazed.

The word *GERMANY* or *Germany* is incised in the base in a straight line about 0.125 inch in height. It is either all capital letters or with a capital *G* and lowercase letters. After the Second World War, the *Germany* stamp was changed to a semicircle phrase *MADE IN GERMANY* or *MADE IN WEST GERMANY.* The model number, if shown, is enclosed within the arc. Any additional stamped or incised number or letter (other than an *A* or *B*) indicates the stein was not made by J. W. Remy.

Hand-drawn ink or hand-scratched marks are often found on the base. These are believed to be marks identifying quality-control or finishing workers. They are sometimes mistakenly interpreted as part of the model number.

Capacity Marks

J. W. Remy marked the capacities on most of its steins. These marks are usually located near the top rim of the stein to the left of the handle attachment. Following the First World War, on steins 1.5 L and larger, the capacities are sometimes inscribed on the base. This is especially characteristic of the vine-accented subgroup.

The company mixed the capacity markings with fractions and decimals. The middle-sized capacities (0.5 L, 0.4 L, and 0.3 L) are represented in decimals rather than fractions. Smaller-sized capacity markings are expressed as fractions, unless they are smaller than 0.125 L. Steins smaller than 0.125 L do not have capacity marks. Capacity marks for steins larger than 1.0 L are represented by whole numbers and fractions. Occasionally, capacity marks will be found incised into the base of postwar steins. For consistency, references within this book to capacity sizes are all noted in decimals.

A feature of this company's decimal markings is that the capacity digits lean to the right, especially the zeros. This characteristic can be an indicator that the piece is likely from J. W. Remy.

Model Numbers

J. W. Remy usually incised model numbers on the base. The physical sizes of incised model numbers are about 0.125 inch to 0.188 inch in height and are italicized. The digits are rarely in-line and have unequal spacing. This indicates the model number stamp was probably composed of separate dies. This may explain occasional errors found in model number marking as well. Building a unique stamp from individual digits would have been a significant cost savings, as opposed to buying or making a unique stamp dedicated for each model.

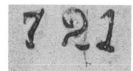   

Model number beside
the lower handle
attachment

Model number
embedded in the
image

Model numbers will occasionally be found embedded in the image on the body and may or may not be repeated on the base. If the model number is a four-digit model and present on the body, there will likely be a five-digit number incised on the base.

The company also generally used different model numbers for different capacities of the same body design. On a few steins, an incised letter *A* or *B* will follow the model number. Instead of assigning a new number, J. W. Remy used the additional letter to denote a different stein capacity of the same design.

Commemorative and souvenir steins are rarely marked with model numbers, although several have assigned numbers in the Model Book. Since these were made for export, all are marked with *Germany* incised in the base.

Last item produced by J. W. Remy
before discontinuing production in 1966

54

CHAPTER 13

CONCLUSION

J. W. Remy produced many diverse wares. Its line of etched steins is distinctive and of high quality. Many of the J. W. Remy designs are unique in the industry.

In the early years of the Golden Age of steins, the company took a significant risk by financing a kiln on J. P. Thewalt's property and shared expertise with that firm. From the late nineteenth century into the first quarter of the twentieth century, J. W. Remy was a leader in the district.

The deaths of the Remy brothers had to have been a shock to the entire village. That event, followed by the Second World War plus increasing competition from overseas, ultimately combined to cause the dissolution of the firm.

PART THREE

Image Catalog

CHAPTER 14

CATALOG OVERVIEW

The following pictorial catalog shows nearly 600 unique steins and other stoneware pieces manufactured by the alliance of J. W. Remy and J. P. Thewalt. Of these, some 160 are etched, and 20 are character steins. There are 21 souvenir or commemorative steins, many of which do not appear in the Model Book. The rest, approximately 400 pieces, are relief steins. Catalog pages, as well as the items they contain, are in ascending order by mold (model) number. The terms model and mold are generally used interchangeably.

Each page shows ten stein images, and each image is captioned with the mold number and capacity of the stein. Text in the lower part of each page provides the mold number, size, style, and a description of the image on each stein.

The descriptions of pieces attributed to J. P. Thewalt include one or more asterisks to indicate the basis for that attribution:

* Marked with the JPT logo
** Pictured in the JPT catalog
*** Mold number conflicts with JWR mold number—*not* JWR

Note that no J. P. Thewalt steins have been identified outside the model number range 1001–1637.

Although the Student series (models 1393–1396) has historically been credited to J. W. Remy, evidence suggests it was probably produced by J. P. Thewalt. No stein from this series has ever been found marked with a logo, none of these steins is pictured in any catalog, and the J. W. Remy Model Book assigns these particular numbers to mustard jars.

Several images on the final pages of the catalog have neither a logo nor a mold number. These pieces have been tentatively attributed to J. W. Remy based upon characteristic similarities to known steins by J. W. Remy.

BELEGSCHAFT DER FIRMA J.W.REMY (CA. 1893)

LINKS: FRANZ REMY
SITZEND 2. VON LINKS: KATHARINA REMY, SPÄTER DIE MUTTER VON
IM DUNKLEN KLEID MIT VASE: KATH. THEWALT   AUGUST, ROBERT, KARL KESSLER
                                         VERH. HIRSCHMANN

Translates as the workforce of the firm J. W. Remy (ca. 1893)
Man standing on left is Franz Remy, son of J. W., second seated woman from left is his sister
Katharina, later the mother of the three Kessler boys who eventually inherited the firm in 1928.

50 0.3 L   52 0.5 L   55 38 CM   111 0.5 L   112 0.5 L

117 0.5 L   128 1.0 L   133 1.5 L   134 1.0 L   135 2.5 L

MOLD	SIZE	STYLE	SCENE
50	0.3 L	RELIEF	Pinten or schnelle style, three scenes, woman, man, *wappen*
52	0.5 L	RELIEF	Pinten or schnelle style, German eagle center cartouche
55	38 CM	RELIEF	Ewer, bacchanalian scene, 1880s
111	0.5 L	RELIEF	Cartouche center flanked by kneeling man and women
112	0.5 L	RELIEF	Small tavern scene, two men, woman, dog
117	0.5 L	THREADED	Mosaic sides and cartouche with saying on front
128	1.0 L	RELIEF	Six knights distributed around body
133	1.5 L	RELIEF	Couples dancing in 1500s dress
134	1.0 L	RELIEF	Bulbous jug, geometrical designs with reverse hearts
135	2.5 L	RELIEF	Detailed relief figures around body with saying interwoven

141 9.75"

143 8.0 L

146 2.5 L

147 5.0 L

152 0.25 L

153
0.25 L

159 4.5 L

185 2.0 L

189 1.5 L

223 13"

MOLD	SIZE	STYLE	SCENE
141	9.75"	RELIEF	Elaborate old style
143	8.0 L	RELIEF	Punchbowl, historismus, cartouches of couples and sayings
146	2.5 L	RELIEF	Two landsknechts holding large center cartouche
147	5.0 L	RELIEF	Four seasons
152	0.25 L	RELIEF	Geometric design
153	0.25 L	RELIEF	Saying on front, banners and fruit on sides
159	4.5 L	RELIEF	Punchbowl, historismus, rococo detail
185	2.0 L	RELIEF	Bulbous four cartouches, old German torsos and heads
189	1.5 L	RELIEF	Threaded relief, deer and bird plus full-relief shield on front
223	13"	RELIEF	Vase, repeating design, six panels, shields, threaded relief

231 1.0 L   232 1.0 L   237 0.25 L   238 0.25 L   240 2.5 L

242 2.0 L   244 3.0 L   247 2.0 L   248 3.0 L   296 0.25 L

MOLD	SIZE	STYLE	SCENE
231	1.0 L	RELIEF	Cartouche, with saying inside and banners
232	1.0 L	RELIEF	Threaded, with cartouche saying on front
237	0.25 L	RELIEF	Three simple shields with sayings
238	0.25 L	RELIEF	Fancy mosaic design with *Hops u Malz, Gott Erhalts*
240	2.5 L	RELIEF	Battle scenes, bulbous shape
242	2.0 L	RELIEF	Bulbous stein with images related to eating food
244	3.0 L	RELIEF	Pitcher with wildman spout and images and sayings
247	2.0 L	RELIEF	Cartouche, sided by two knights, bulbous shape, no capacity
248	3.0 L	RELIEF	Bulbous, five large cartouches, wild man spout
296	0.25 L	RELIEF	Historismus style

| 297 0.25 L | 298 0.25 L | 299 0.25 L | 307 0.5 L | 312 0.5 L |

| 313 0.5 L | 314 0.5 L | 315 0.5 L | 321 23 CM | 330 1.0 Kg |

MOLD	SIZE	STYLE	SCENE
297	0.25 L	RELIEF	Bulbous, repeating design
298	0.25 L	RELIEF	Cartouch center, flanked by kneeling man and women
299	0.25 L	RELIEF	Front cartouche "A good drink makes old young"
307	0.5 L	RELIEF	Banner on front, griffins on each side
312	0.5 L	RELIEF	Flat base, cartouche on front of father Jahn, 4F on sides
313	0.5 L	RELIEF	Flat base, saying on front with images on sides
314	0.5 L	RELIEF	Flat base, three dancing couples and flute player on barrel
315	0.5 L	RELIEF	Threaded, flat base, *Prosit*, face, mosaic design
321	23 CM	RELIEF	Vase, four heads in profile on body
330	1.0 Kg	RELIEF	Tobacco jar, several cartouches on body

331 1.0 Kg

340 3.0 L

341 3.0 L

343 1.5 L

344 2.0 L

348 1.5 L

349 1.5 L

350 7.75"

371 0.3 L

374 0.5 L

MOLD	SIZE	STYLE	SCENE
331	1.0 Kg	RELIEF	Tobacco jar, series of knights from 1500s
340	3.0 L	RELIEF	Four standing women
341	3.0 L	RELIEF	Threaded, fancy saying, mosaic design
343	1.5 L	RELIEF	Two Roman centurions seated on brick wall
344	2.0 L	RELIEF	Saying with knights in cartouches on each side
348	1.5 L	RELIEF	Historismus, eight cartouches of popes
349	1.5 L	RELIEF	Pitcher, three couples, flute player, geometric design
350	7.75"	RELIEF	Mosaic, threaded
371	0.3 L	RELIEF	Gasthaus scene, seated man with barmaid, hugging
374	0.5 L	RELIEF	Two Bavarian cartouches with saying around base

| 377 0.5 L | 382 0.5 L | 391 0.3 L | 394 0.25 L | 400 14.75 L |

409 4.0 L   410 3.0 L   427 0.5 L   428 0.5 L   429 0.5 L

MOLD	SIZE	STYLE	SCENE
377	0.5 L	RELIEF	Three at table in gasthaus, two men courting seated woman
382	0.5 L	RELIEF	Seated man and standing woman in renaissance dress
391	0.3 L	RELIEF	Cartouche with saying plus two renaissance figures
394	0.25 L	RELIEF	Cherubs and floating steins
400	14.75 L	RELIEF	Barrel wrapped with grapes and leaves
409	4.0 L	RELIEF	Punchbowl, dwarfs
410	3.0 L	RELIEF	Two women, one man in renaissance dress, pitcher style
427	0.5 L	RELIEF	Oval saying on front, two figures on sides
428	0.5 L	RELIEF	Two cavalier side cartouches, plus saying on front
429	0.5 L	RELIEF	Two putti in cartouche

430 4.0 L   431 2.0 L   432 2.5 L   440 1.0 L   441 1.0 L

443 1.0 L   468 2.5 L   471 0.3 L   473 0.25 L   476 1.0 L

MOLD	SIZE	STYLE	SCENE
430	4.0 L	RELIEF	Cartouches of two courting couples plus phrase on front
431	2.0 L	RELIEF	Musical motif
432	2.5 L	RELIEF	Castles with phrases, man and woman, figures on sides
440	1.0 L	RELIEF	Four people on front, two cartouches with text on sides
441	1.0 L	RELIEF	Gasthaus, two men, one woman seated, one man standing
443	1.0 L	RELIEF	Two lions on cartouche of *Prosit*
468	2.5 L	RELIEF	Cartouches, musicians, devil spout, master 0.3 L steins, 531
471	0.3 L	RELIEF	Four cartouches on body of two couples facing
473	0.25 L	RELIEF	Four cartouches including *Lanzelot* (Lancelot)
476	1.0 L	RELIEF	Tavern scene, two men, woman seated plus one standing

478 1.0 L   480 1.0 L   483 1.0 L   486 0.5 L   488 0.5 L

491 1.5 L   492 2.0 L   493 2.0 L   494 2.0 L   496 5.0 L

MOLD	SIZE	STYLE	SCENE
478	1.0 L	RELIEF	Tavern scene, seated man, woman standing drinking
480	1.0 L	ETCHED	Schlitt-style, gnome in nest, no color
483	1.0 L	RELIEF	Seated man with zither beside woman, same as 1217
486	0.5 L	RELIEF	Two putti inside cartouche on front
488	0.5 L	RELIEF	Stylized face on front, mosaic
491	1.5 L	RELIEF	Three cartouches of two cherubs
492	2.0 L	RELIEF	4-F tankard
493	2.0 L	RELIEF	Late 1700s style, two couples on side, saying center
494	2.0 L	RELIEF	Several cartouches with putti
496	5.0 L	RELIEF	Saying on front, with shell cartouches

| 497 4.0 L | 498 2.0 L | 499 3.0 L | 505 0.5 L | 519 1.0 L |

| 522 0.5 L | 523 0.5 L | 524 0.5 L | 525 0.5 L | 528 0.3 L |

MOLD	SIZE	STYLE	SCENE
497	4.0 L	RELIEF	Three statues with historismus style
498	2.0 L	RELIEF	Seated musician with mandolin and stein
499	3.0 L	RELIEF	The Flirt
505	0.5 L	RELIEF	Two putti, with tree and firewood
519	1.0 L	RELIEF	Woman serving food to three at table
522	0.5 L	RELIEF	Woman riding bicycle
523	0.5 L	RELIEF	*Jaeger Latein*, three seated with maid standing
524	0.5 L	RELIEF	Gasthaus scene, maid bringing three steins of beer
525	0.5 L	RELIEF	Man, woman courting, seated
528	0.3 L	RELIEF	Small cartouche on front and man and woman on sides

528 0.3 L

529 0.3 L

531 0.3 L

533 0.25 L

540 2.0 L

541 3.0 L

542 1.5 L

543 3.0 L

544 2.0 L

545 1.5 L

MOLD	SIZE	STYLE	SCENE
528	0.3 L	RELIEF	Small cartouche on front and man and woman on sides
529	0.3 L	RELIEF	Cartouche, *Dein Wohl*, set of four, matches 467 The Flirt
531	0.3 L	RELIEF	Geometric or flowers
533	0.25 L	RELIEF	Renaissance side cartouches
540	2.0 L	RELIEF	Kneeling man wooing woman seated on balustrade
541	3.0 L	RELIEF	Cherubs and seasons in cartouches
542	1.5 L	RELIEF	Two men, one seated woman knitting
543	3.0 L	RELIEF	Two couples from late 1700s
544	2.0 L	RELIEF	Zither player with woman
545	1.5 L	RELIEF	Gambrinus on barrel, toasting, lots of hops and leaves

546 2.0 L   547 1.5 L   549 5.0 L   550 2.0 Kg   554 0.5 L

555 0.5 L   560 1.0 L   561 1.0 L   563 1.0 L   564 1.0 L

MOLD	SIZE	STYLE	SCENE
546	2.0 L	RELIEF	Bicyclist
547	1.5 L	RELIEF	Two musicians and saying on front
549	5.0 L	RELIEF	Historismus, man, woman side cartouches, phrase on front
550	2.0 Kg	RELIEF	Tobacco jar, typical putti cartouches
554	0.5 L	RELIEF	Cartouch with saying on front
555	0.5 L	RELIEF	Bowling scene
560	1.0 L	RELIEF	Paying the bill
561	1.0 L	RELIEF	Zither player with woman, recessed base
563	1.0 L	RELIEF	Cartouche on front with saying, two dwarves on sides
564	1.0 L	RELIEF	Seated man with mandolin

565 1.0 L

566 1.0 L

568 1.0 L

579 0.5 L

580 1.5 L

585 0.5 L

599 2.0 L

600 2.0 L

606 2.0 L

610 1.0 L

MOLD	SIZE	STYLE	SCENE
565	1.0 L	RELIEF	Gasthaus, two seated men and barmaid with filled steins
566	1.0 L	RELIEF	Two men and one woman seated
568	1.0 L	RELIEF	Two women, one man at table watching child drink
579	0.5 L	RELIEF	Two women, one man in gasthaus, same scene as 568
580	1.5 L	RELIEF	Tavern scene, bulbous base, brewer's stars around base
585	0.5 L	RELIEF	Barmaid delivering to two gentlemen sitting in gasthaus
599	2.0 L	RELIEF	Gasthaus scene, *Jager Sasein*, storytelling
600	2.0 L	RELIEF	Historismus, bulbous, two large cartouches on sides
606	2.0 L	RELIEF	Historismus, cartouches around bulbous base
610	1.0 L	RELIEF	Tavern scene, woman standing, three men

611 1.0 L

612 1.0 L

613 1.0 L

614 1.0 L

615 2.0 L

616 3.0 L

617 4.0 L

617 5.0 L

618 1.5 L

619 2.0 L

MOLD	SIZE	STYLE	SCENE
611	1.0 L	RELIEF	Two men, one woman seated outside
612	1.0 L	RELIEF	Mandolin player
613	1.0 L	RELIEF	Munich Child
614	1.0 L	RELIEF	Adults seated, child drinking
615	2.0 L	RELIEF	Large gasthaus scene with nine men, a waitress, a dog
616	3.0 L	RELIEF	Large gashouse scene, many people
617	4.0 L	RELIEF	Gasthaus scene, banjo player and two men around a barrel
617	5.0 L	RELIEF	Gasthaus scene, same scene as 4.0 L version above
618	1.5 L	RELIEF	Man in seventeenth-century dress courting coy woman
619	2.0 L	RELIEF	Woman, hunter, three dogs at closed door

623 0.5 Kg

636 0.5 L

638 0.5 L

641 0.5 L

650 22"

651 1.0 L

653 0.125 L

655 1.0 L

656 2.5 L

659 0.25 L

MOLD	SIZE	STYLE	SCENE
623	0.5 Kg	RELIEF	Historismus, two renaissance figures
636	0.5 L	RELIEF	Celebrating cavaliers
638	0.5 L	RELIEF	Early Germans, woodland scene, helmet with wings
641	0.5 L	RELIEF	Man on bicycle
650	22"	RELIEF	Large umbrella stand
651	1.0 L	RELIEF	Zither player with girlfriend
653	0.125 L	RELIEF	Mustard jar, diamond design
655	1.0 L	RELIEF	Outdoor large celebration
656	2.5 L	RELIEF	Front view of three cavaliers partying around a table
659	0.25 L	RELIEF	*In Freud und Leid*, *Treu Jederzeit*, with flowers

74

660 0.5 L

670 3.0 L

671 2.0 L

672 1.5 L

673 1.5 L

675 1.0 L

678 1.0 L

687 0.5 L

689 0.5 L

699 0.5 L

MOLD	SIZE	STYLE	SCENE
660	0.5 L	RELIEF	Cavalier on white horse
670	3.0 L	RELIEF	Gasthaus scene, banjo player and two men around a barrel
671	2.0 L	RELIEF	Munich Child, *Hofbrauhaus*, highly detailed
672	1.5 L	RELIEF	Zither player with seated woman
673	1.5 L	RELIEF	Tavern with violinist playing
675	1.0 L	RELIEF/DECAL	Gasthaus dance scene
678	1.0 L	RELIEF	Three cartouches, Trumpeter of Säckingen
687	0.5 L	RELIEF	Monkeys on a tree
689	0.5 L	RELIEF	Cartouche with roses on sides, unusual green glaze
699	0.5 L	RELIEF	Wilhelm Tell

706 0.5 L

707 0.5 L

709 0.25 L

711 1.0 L

713 0.25 L

717 1.0 L

720 5.0 L

721 5.0 L

722 3.0 L

723 1.5 L

MOLD	SIZE	STYLE	SCENE
706	0.5 L	RELIEF	Hiker waving handkerchief
707	0.5 L	RELIEF	Soccer player kicking ball
709	0.25 L	RELIEF	Three cavaliers, one with mandolin, has pour spout
711	1.0 L	RELIEF	*Landsknecht* with standing, drinking maiden (marked 478)
713	0.25 L	RELIEF	Gasthaus scene, two men at table
717	1.0 L	ETCHED	Gasthaus scene, gentleman entertaining group of five
720	5.0 L	RELIEF	Norse hunter blowing horn in forest
721	5.0 L	ETCHED	Farm scene with farmer wiping forehead in foreground
722	3.0 L	ETCHED	Farm scene with sheep in foreground
723	1.5 L	ETCHED	Sheep with farm scene in background

724 4.0 L   725 2.0 L   727 4.0 L   728 2.5 L   729 3.0 L

729 3.0 L   730 0.5 L   731 0.5 L   732 0.25 L   733 0.5 L

MOLD	SIZE	STYLE	SCENE
724	4.0 L	ETCHED	Farm horses pulling farm wagon
725	2.0 L	ETCHED	Two farm girls with sheep
727	4.0 L	RELIEF	Tavern scene, dancer, *Holzerschmarren*
728	2.5 L	RELIEF	Gasthaus scene, dancer
729	3.0 L	RELIEF	Six people in outdoor drinking scene
729	3.0 L	RELIEF	Six people in outdoor drinking scene, rare color combination
730	0.5 L	ETCHED	*A Lustig's Liedl*, two men and a woman at a table
731	0.5 L	ETCHED	Keller scene, women, guitarist, *Der Schnadaheupfl Sepp*
732	0.25 L	ETCHED	Guitarist serenading a couple
733	0.5 L	ETCHED	*Erinnerung Wandern*, remembering a hike

736 0.25 L

737 0.25 L

741 0.5 L

748 0.5 L

751 2.5 L

752 0.3 L

753 1.0 L

754 1.0 L

755 1.0 L

756 1.0 L

MOLD	SIZE	STYLE	SCENE
736	0.25 L	ETCHED	Seven people, tavern scene, incorrectly marked 786
737	0.25 L	ETCHED	Outdoor drinking scene, two seated men, bartender
741	0.5 L	RELIEF	Renaissance couple by lake, Swedish text, dual mark 1238
748	0.5 L	RELIEF	Two farmers and farming scene on side and back
751	2.5 L	RELIEF	Outdoor dancing scene with seated musicians
752	0.3 L	RELIEF	Large group outdoors, Good Times
753	1.0 L	RELIEF	Gasthaus scene, *Festessen*, flat base
754	1.0 L	RELIEF	Home scene of *Jäger* teaching boy to shoot rifle
755	1.0 L	RELIEF	Home scene with kids and dogs
756	1.0 L	RELIEF	*Festessen*, same scene as 753 with hollow base

| 758 1.5 L | 761 0.25 Kg | 764 1.0 Kg | 765 0.5 L | 766 0.5 L |

| 767 0.5 L | 768 0.5 L | 769 0.5 L | 770 0.5 L | 773 0.3 L |

MOLD	SIZE	STYLE	SCENE
758	1.5 L	RELIEF	Hunter and two maidens, *Absheid*
761	0.25 Kg	RELIEF	Snuff jar, three cartouches of faces
764	1.0 Kg	RELIEF	Tobacco jar, celebrating musketeers
765	0.5 L	CHARACTER	Gentleman with music box base
766	0.5 L	CHARACTER	Gentlewoman with flower in mouth, salt glaze example
767	0.5 L	CHARACTER	Gentleman cat
768	0.5 L	CHARACTER	Gentleman dog dressed as hunter
769	0.5 L	CHARACTER	Military monkey
770	0.5 L	CHARACTER	Gentleman pig with bag of money
773	0.3 L	RELIEF	Two couples and guitar player seated outside

774 0.25 L

775 0.25 L

776 6.0 L

777 2.0 L

778 4.0 L

779 1.5 L

780 0.125 L

782 0.125 L

783 0.125 L

789 0.5 L

MOLD	SIZE	STYLE	SCENE
774	0.25 L	CHARACTER	Cat with bowl
775	0.25 L	CHARACTER	Rabbit with tennis racquet
776	6.0 L	RELIEF	*Der Aschenspieler*, large gasthaus scene
777	2.0 L	RELIEF	Two maids, one man, playing *fingernageln*
778	4.0 L	RELIEF	Outdoor scene, group welcoming riders home
779	1.5 L	RELIEF	*Schneewittchen*, Snow White and prince, four dwarfs
780	0.125 L	RELIEF	Clover leaves, *Viel Gluck* on front
782	0.125 L	RELIEF	*Dornroschen*, spinning wheel, Sleeping Beauty
783	0.125 L	RELIEF	Snow White with all seven dwarves
789	0.5 L	RELIEF	Subset of *Sitz die hier* scene

| 791 0.5 L | 792 0.5 L | 793 1.0 L | 794 1.0 L | 801 0.25 L |

| 813 0.4 L | 819 0.3 L | 821 0.5 L | 823 0.5 L | 824 0.5 L |

MOLD	SIZE	STYLE	SCENE
791	0.5 L	RELIEF	Outdoor group, family party
792	0.5 L	RELIEF	Soldier astride horse
793	1.0 L	RELIEF	Bull riding in Tirol
794	1.0 L	RELIEF	Outdoor tavern, angry man pointing at another
801	0.25 L	RELIEF	Maid waiting on seated cavalier
813	0.4 L	RELIEF	Hunter leaving his girl, flat base
819	0.3 L	RELIEF	Tavern scene, three men sitting, woman standing
821	0.5 L	RELIEF	Bowling scene, woman bowling
823	0.5 L	RELIEF	Teaching woman to ride a bicycle
824	0.5 L	RELIEF	Three in a gasthaus playing instruments at a table

825 0.5 L

826 0.5 L

827 0.5 L

828 0.5 L

829 0.5 L

838 12"

839 12"

842 2.5 L

843 7.0 L

844 2.0 L

MOLD	SIZE	STYLE	SCENE
825	0.5 L	RELIEF	Man on boat shaking hands with maiden on dock
826	0.5 L	RELIEF	1700s man courting woman
827	0.5 L	RELIEF	Woman bowling
828	0.5 L	ETCHED	Faust and Gretchen
829	0.5 L	ETCHED	Mandolin player with women and children
838	12"	RELIEF	Plaque, outdoor argument similar to 794
839	12"	RELIEF	Plaque, *holzerschmarren*, outdoor dancer and partiers
842	2.5 L	RELIEF	*Gasthaus* scene, man making pass at maiden
843	7.0 L	RELIEF	Large outdoor bowling party
844	2.0 L	RELIEF	Five in tavern, one toasting viewer, available as part of a set

| 845 2.5 L | 846 1.5 L | 847 2.0 L | 848 3.0 L | 849 1.5 L |

| 854 0.25 L | 855 1.0 L | 860 0.5 L | 861 0.5 L | 862 1.0 L |

MOLD	SIZE	STYLE	SCENE
845	2.5 L	RELIEF	Three seated women rocking with two seated gentlemen
846	1.5 L	ETCHED	Couple on horses with dog, beautiful sunset scene
847	2.0 L	ETCHED	Three people at a table, a man toasting a young girl
848	3.0 L	ETCHED	Guitar player in gasthaus scene
849	1.5 L	RELIEF	Gasthaus scene, two seated and a standing waitress
854	0.25 L	ETCHED	Two 1700s men toasting at table
855	1.0 L	ETCHED	Ladies listening to musician
860	0.5 L	RELIEF	1700s couple sitting outdoors on large rock
861	0.5 L	RELIEF	Two seated drinkers plus barmaid in keller open to sky
862	1.0 L	RELIEF	Outdoor, 1700s couple, man courting young maiden

863 1.0 L

866 1.0 L

871 2.0 Kg

873 3.0 L

874 2.5 L

875 1.5 L

876 1.5 L

877 1.5 L

878 3.0 L

880 0.25 L

MOLD	SIZE	STYLE	SCENE
863	1.0 L	RELIEF	Outdoor four-person group scene
866	1.0 L	ETCHED	Gasthaus scene
871	2.0 Kg	RELIEF	Tobacco jar, *landsknecht* on horse plus men on foot
873	3.0 L	RELIEF	Man sitting on stump, seated woman sewing
874	2.5 L	RELIEF	Gasthaus scene, three seated, man dancing, woman serving
875	1.5 L	RELIEF	*Auf der Alm*, outdoor scene
876	1.5 L	RELIEF	*Das Kellerfest*, 1700s dress
877	1.5 L	RELIEF	Family at table with maid holding baby
878	3.0 L	RELIEF	Tavern scene, *Ein Schelmenlied*
880	0.25 L	RELIEF	Five in tavern, one toasting viewer

882 0.3 L

883 0.4 L

884 0.5 L

887 0.5 L

888 0.5 L

889 0.5 L

895 0.5 L

896 0.5 L

899 0.5 L

900 1.0 L

MOLD	SIZE	STYLE	SCENE
882	0.3 L	ETCHED	Outdoor scene, woman on wall with man behind
883	0.4 L	ETCHED	Gasthaus scene, waitress dancing, man singing, man playing
884	0.5 L	ETCHED	Three musicians at table
887	0.5 L	RELIEF	Nineteenth-century lovers by pond with geese
888	0.5 L	RELIEF	Czech, "God, I love beer," three people
889	0.5 L	RELIEF	Man and two seated women, Czech language
895	0.5 L	RELIEF	*Das Kellerfest*
896	0.5 L	ETCHED	Knight on white spotted horse
899	0.5 L	ETCHED	Knights stealing cows, then captured
900	1.0 L	CHARACTER	Munich Child

901 0.5 L   905 0.5 L   906 0.5 L   907 0.4 L   908 0.3 L

909 0.25 L   911 0.5 L   912 0.5 L   913 0.5 L   915 0.5 L

MOLD	SIZE	STYLE	SCENE
901	0.5 L	CHARACTER	Munich Child
905	0.5 L	ETCHED AND RELIEF	Man and two women all seated *Ein Prieschen gefallig*
906	0.5 L	ETCHED	*Lohengrin's Abschied*, swan and boat
907	0.4 L	ETCHED	Two men seated in gasthaus, one with cigar
908	0.3 L	ETCHED	Two 1700s seated men watching two maidens
909	0.25 L	ETCHED	Kellerer standing by barrel with seated customer
911	0.5 L	ETCHED	Renaissance man and woman on porch, musicians
912	0.5 L	ETCHED AND RELIEF	*Schwazer Peter*, gasthaus scene with several card players
913	0.5 L	RELIEF	Seidel, recessed base, *Jetz geh I aus Brummele*
915	0.5 L	RELIEF	*Trompeters Liebesheid,* woman holding ears

916 0.5 L

918 0.5 L

920 2.0 L

921 1.5 L

923 2.0 L

924 2.5 L

925 1.0 L

926 1.0 L

927 1.0 L

928 1.0 L

MOLD	SIZE	STYLE	SCENE
916	0.5 L	RELIEF	Seated alpine couple, with a pipe
918	0.5 L	RELIEF	Boy and girl courting while father looks on
920	2.0 L	RELIEF	Family scene around table with three puppies on table
921	1.5 L	RELIEF	1700s couple in woods, reading
923	2.0 L	ETCHED	Keller scene with drunks and friar
924	2.5 L	RELIEF	Tavern, two men and barmaid with pigeon
925	1.0 L	ETCHED AND RELIEF	Tavern, two women, hunter, three dogs
926	1.0 L	RELIEF	Two hunters, deer, fox, eagle, pheasant
927	1.0 L	ETCHED AND RELIEF	Tavern, *Wilderer in der Sennhutte*
928	1.0 L	ETCHED	Two cavaliers and woman seated at table

| 929 1.0 L | 932 1.5 L | 934 1.0 L | 935 3.0 L | 936 2.0 L |

| 937 10.0 L | 938 2.0 L | 939 3.0 L | 940 0.5 L | 942 0.5 L |

MOLD	SIZE	STYLE	SCENE
929	1.0 L	ETCHED	Gasthaus, four men, one woman, *Im Herrenstubchen*
932	1.5 L	RELIEF	Four at table, man handing woman cup, multiple sizes
934	1.0 L	RELIEF	Andreas Hofer scene
935	3.0 L	RELIEF	Outdoor scene with band on balcony and dancers
936	2.0 L	RELIEF	Tavern scene, *Beim Tanz*
937	10.0 L	RELIEF	Couple in cavalier dress, he has a large glass of beer
938	2.0 L	RELIEF	Outdoor scene, man feeding a woman with a spoon
939	3.0 L	RELIEF	Norseman blowing horn
940	0.5 L	RELIEF	Couple playing chess
942	0.5 L	RELIEF	Six people seated outdoors, part of Fun Times set

943 0.5 L

946 1.0 L

947 1.0 L

948 1.0 L

949 1.0 L

950 0.5 L

951 0.5 L

954 0.5 L

958 0.25 L

960 1.5 L

MOLD	SIZE	STYLE	SCENE
943	0.5 L	ETCHED	The clock at 1:00, recessed base
946	1.0 L	ETCHED	Three women, seated man with lute and bartender
947	1.0 L	ETCHED	Monks at dinner
948	1.0 L	RELIEF	Three seated men focused on woman, maid standing behind
949	1.0 L	ETCHED	Large cartouche, man and woman toasting wine
950	0.5 L	RELIEF	Couple seated at barrel, the man has an arm around the maid
951	0.5 L	ETCHED	Horse riders and man posing with deer
954	0.5 L	ETCHED	The Surprised Knight
958	0.25 L	ETCHED	The Surprised Knight
960	1.5 L	ETCHED	Gasthaus scene

| 961 2.0 L | 962 2.5 L | 964 1.5 L | 965 20.0 L | 966 1.5 L |

| 967 1.5 L | 969 2.0 L | 970 0.5 L | 972 0.5 L | 973 0.5 L |

MOLD	SIZE	STYLE	SCENE
961	2.0 L	ETCHED	Wealthy gentlemen in keller, wine tasting
962	2.5 L	ETCHED	Guitarist serenading two sitting women and man
964	1.5 L	ETCHED	The Surprised Knight
965	20.0 L	RELIEF	Three German kings, heavy relief, missing set-on lid
966	1.5 L	RELIEF	Three cavaliers seated by barrel outdoors
967	1.5 L	RELIEF	Hunter and dog returning with deer slung over shoulders
969	2.0 L	RELIEF	*Jaeger* (hunter) giving seated woman flowers
970	0.5 L	RELIEF	Colorful soldiers being treated by young woman
972	0.5 L	CHARACTER	Ram or bock
973	0.5 L	CHARACTER	Frog

976 0.5 L

978 0.5 L

979 0.5 L

980 0.5 L

990 1.0 L

991 1.0 L

1004 0.5 L*

1009 1.0 L

1009 0.4 L**

1010 0.5 L

MOLD	SIZE	STYLE	SCENE
976	0.5 L	CHARACTER	Pinecone
978	0.5 L	RELIEF	Maiden in forest dreaming at table
979	0.5 L	RELIEF	Zither player and dancers
980	0.5 L	ETCHED	Group hike in forest
990	1.0 L	RELIEF	Bavarian scene, man and four young women
991	1.0 L	RELIEF	Two men, one woman seated at table in gasthaus
1004	0.5 L	RELIEF	Guitar player and two friends, *
1009	1.0 L	ETCHED	Card game, *Schwazer Peter*
1009	0.4 L	RELIEF	Cartouche of man toasting, **
1010	0.5 L	ETCHED	Gasthaus, three men seated, two standing

| 1011 0.5 L | 1011 0.5 L** | 1012 0.5 L | 1016 0.5 L | 1025 0.5 L* |

| 1027 1.5 L* | 1030 1.0 L* | 1033 1.0 L* | 1034 1.0 L* | 1037 1.0 L* |

MOLD	SIZE	STYLE	SCENE
1011	0.5 L	ETCHED	Woman, man by brick wall, man drinking out of jug
1011	0.5 L	RELIEF	Village scene with house, church, and hills, **
1012	0.5 L	ETCHED	Barmaid leaning over a shoulder of a writer
1016	0.5 L	ETCHED	Art deco, unusual English inscription, mismarked 1116
1025	0.5 L	RELIEF	Mandolin player with seated man and standing woman, *
1027	1.5 L	RELIEF	Man and woman playing cards, man and woman watching, *
1030	1.0 L	RELIEF	Young couple with girl at table, inside a cartouche, *
1033	1.0 L	RELIEF	Munich Child before and after, with saying on front, *
1034	1.0 L	RELIEF	Three guys sitting at a table, smoking and drinking, *
1037	1.0 L	RELIEF	Keller scene with four people, *

1042 1.0 L

1045 0.3 L*

1045 1.0 L*

1046 0.25 L**

1049 1.0 L

1058 0.25 L**

1059 0.75 L

1062 2.0 L

1066 2.0 L**

1067 2.0 L

MOLD	SIZE	STYLE	SCENE
1042	1.0 L	RELIEF	Stag or elk on front
1045	0.3 L	RELIEF	Musical instruments around body, *
1045	1.0 L	RELIEF	Hermann with harpist, woman, and soldier, * (mismarked)
1046	0.25 L	RELIEF	Two shields on front with crosses, **
1049	1.0 L	RELIEF	*Lustige Gesellschaft*
1058	0.25 L	RELIEF	Renaissance horseman and dogs chasing deer, **
1059	0.75 L	RELIEF	Leupold von Dessau, horsemen
1062	2.0 L	RELIEF	Rum pot
1066	2.0 L	RELIEF	Pitcher, hunting scene with bands of flowers, **
1067	2.0 L	ETCHED	Cavaliers and woman, high decorated bands, also as 11067

1079 0.3 L	1080 2.0 L**	1085 2.0 L*	1086 2.0 L*	1086 1.0 L

1087 3.0 L*	1087 1.0 L	1088 3.0 L*	1094 1.5 L	1102 0.5 L*

MOLD	SIZE	STYLE	SCENE
1079	0.3 L	ETCHED	Dutch scene
1080	2.0 L	RELIEF	Musical score in center and two musicians on side, **
1085	2.0 L	RELIEF	Cavalier and barmaid inside a cartouche, *
1086	2.0 L	RELIEF	People riding on train, *
1086	1.0 L	RELIEF	Happy and friendly scene, sitting and drinking
1087	3.0 L	RELIEF	*Der schmied der Deutscher Einheit*, Brunhilde, *
1087	1.0 L	RELIEF	Cavaliers seated at barrel with mugs and waitress
1088	3.0 L	RELIEF	Gasthaus scene, three men, one woman all seated, *
1094	1.5 L	ETCHED	Dutch scene, also as 11094
1102	0.5 L	RELIEF	Seated man with standing woman, drinking, *

| 1104 0.5 L* | 1104 0.5 L | 1105 0.5 L | 1110 0.5 L | 1111 0.75 L |

| 1113 0.75 L | 1116 0.75 L | 1118 0.5 L* | 1121 1.5 L | 1123 2.0 L |

MOLD	SIZE	STYLE	SCENE
1104	0.5 L	RELIEF	*Nach Dem Konzert*, two standing musicians drinking, *
1104	0.5 L	RELIEF	Chess pieces and board
1105	0.5 L	RELIEF	Outdoor scene, four men in renaissance dress drinking
1110	0.5 L	RELIEF	Gasthaus scene, maid bringing a dish of food to table
1111	0.75 L	RELIEF	Germans introducing beer to Roman soldiers
1113	0.75 L	RELIEF	Renaissance scene, two mandolins, cavalier toasting
1116	0.75 L	RELIEF	Fisherman showing fish to girl with several onlookers
1118	0.5 L	RELIEF	Bavarian couple inside plain cartouche, *
1121	1.5 L	RELIEF	Medieval dance scene
1123	2.0 L	RELIEF	Two men seated, standing woman with horn

1126 2.0 L

1127 0.5 L*

1142 2.0 L*

1144 0.5 L*

1147 0.5 L***

1158 0.5 L*

1159 0.4 L*

1160 0.4 L*

1166 0.5 L***

1168 2.0 L

MOLD	SIZE	STYLE	SCENE
1126	2.0 L	RELIEF	Outdoor target shoot
1127	0.5 L	RELIEF	Man and woman holding hands, *
1142	2.0 L	RELIEF	Six scenes of occupations, *
1144	0.5 L	RELIEF	1600s tavern scene, *
1147	0.5 L	RELIEF	Waterwheel, correct handle, hollow base, ***
1158	0.5 L	RELIEF	Two standing cavalier musicians, *
1159	0.4 L	RELIEF	Several dwarves with saying on bottom, *
1160	0.4 L	RELIEF	Three cartouches, musketeer drinking with stein, *
1166	0.5 L	RELIEF	Sitting man beside artesian well under tree, ***
1168	2.0 L	RELIEF	Two couples courting, and zither player, vine style

1171 0.5 L**

1173 0.5 L***

1175 0.5 L*

1179 0.5 L

1180 0.5 L**

1189 0.5 L

1196 0.5 L*

1197 0.5 L

1204 6.0 L*

1205 4.0 L*

MOLD	SIZE	STYLE	SCENE
1171	0.5 L	RELIEF	Dancing frogs, **
1173	0.5 L	RELIEF	1700s couple in woods, woman crying, ***
1175	0.5 L	RELIEF	Two women and one man, woman lighting man's cigar, *
1179	0.5 L	ETCHED	Bowling scene
1180	0.5 L	RELIEF	Hand-painted man and dog in forest, tree trunk style, **
1189	0.5 L	RELIEF	Two dancers, man with zither, woman, vine style
1196	0.5 L	RELIEF	Three-handled pass cup, hunter and dog after two *chamois*, *
1197	0.5 L	RELIEF	Couple plus woman and hunter with pheasant
1204	6.0 L	RELIEF	Outdoor tavern scene with card players, *
1205	4.0 L	RELIEF	Cavalier couple hugging, *

1206 4.0 L*

1208 0.5 L*

1209 0.5 L***

1210 0.5 L*

1211 1.0 L*

1212 2.5 L***

1213 1.5 L**

1214 3.0 L***

1214 1.5 L

1216 1.5 L

MOLD	SIZE	STYLE	SCENE
1206	4.0 L	RELIEF	1600s man with flute, seated woman with mandolin, *
1208	0.5 L	ETCHED	Woods scene, hunter nuzzling maid, *
1209	0.5 L	ETCHED	Hunter and maiden with target, ***
1210	0.5 L	ETCHED	*Das Märchen*, *
1211	1.0 L	ETCHED	Gasthaus, two men and woman plus woman zither player, *
1212	2.5 L	ETCHED	Hunter showing off his kills to two women and kids, ***
1213	1.5 L	ETCHED	Tavern scene, man and woman musicians, woman at fire, **
1214	3.0 L	ETCHED	Outdoor mountain scene, two maidens and a hiker, ***
1214	1.5 L	RELIEF	Outdoor stag scene
1216	1.5 L	RELIEF	Outdoors, lady and four men at table

1217 0.5 L*   1218 0.5 L***   1220 0.5 L***   1221 0.5 L***   1221 0.5 L*

1222 1.0 L*   1223 2.0 L***   1224 1.5 L*   1225 1.0 L***   1226 0.25 L*

MOLD	SIZE	STYLE	SCENE
1217	0.5 L	ETCHED AND RELIEF	Seated man with zither beside woman, like 483, *
1218	0.5 L	ETCHED	Men toasting and man and woman dancing outdoors, ***
1220	0.5 L	ETCHED	Renaissance scene with fortune-teller and men, ***
1221	0.5 L	ETCHED	Seated fat man pointing at man standing up, ***
1221	0.5 L	ETCHED	Rare salt glaze fired, same scene as above, *
1222	1.0 L	ETCHED	Keller scene with several cavaliers, *
1223	2.0 L	ETCHED	Gasthaus scene, five men in 1500s dress, with steins, ***
1224	1.5 L	ETCHED	Renaissance hunters, *
1225	1.0 L	ETCHED	Knight with maiden seated on upholstered bench, ***
1226	0.25 L	ETCHED	Two men seated drinking beer, one with mandolin, *

1227 0.5 L*

1228 0.5 L***

1229 0.5 L***

1235 1.0 L*

1236 0.5 L

1238 0.5 L*

1243 0.5 L*

1280 2.0 L*

1288 0.3 L

1291 0.5 L*

MOLD	SIZE	STYLE	SCENE
1227	0.5 L	ETCHED	Five cavaliers in tavern, one with mandolin, *
1228	0.5 L	RELIEF	Courting couple, renaissance dress, ***
1229	0.5 L	RELIEF	Seated musketeer serenading maiden with lute, ***
1235	1.0 L	RELIEF	Pass cup, three renaissance scenes, *
1236	0.5 L	CHARACTER	Jugendstil bowling ball
1238	0.5 L	RELIEF	Couple by lake, Swedish phrase, dual marked 741, *
1243	0.5 L	RELIEF	Target stein, *
1280	2.0 L	ETCHED	Punch bowl, likely Karl Goerig design in blue-green, *
1288	0.3 L	RELIEF	Seated cavalier and maiden leaning against each other
1291	0.5 L	ETCHED	Seated man with mandolin serenading woman, *

1292 0.5 L***

1293 0.25 L*

1294 0.4 L***

1295 0.3 L***

1296 1.0 L*

1297 0.4 L***

1299 0.5 L

1308 0.5 L

1322 0.5 L

1333 1.0 L***

MOLD	SIZE	STYLE	SCENE
1292	0.5 L	ETCHED	Gasthaus scene, standing man courting seated woman, ***
1293	0.25 L	ETCHED	Man and woman seated in keller drinking wine, *
1294	0.4 L	ETCHED	Maid waiting on seated cavalier, ***
1295	0.3 L	ETCHED	Glutton in a cellar, possible Gambrinus, ***
1296	1.0 L	ETCHED	Cavaliers partying in keller, discovered by monk, *
1297	0.4 L	ETCHED	Renaissance man playing music for woman, ***
1299	0.5 L	CHARACTER	Tower with clock faces, cat handle
1308	0.5 L	RELIEF	King of gnomes plus several bands of gnomes around
1322	0.5 L	RELIEF	Renaissance man and woman holding hands, saying
1333	1.0 L	ETCHED	Seated man talking to two seated women, ***

1334 0.5 L***

1335 0.5 L***

1336 1.0 L***

1337 0.5 L***

1338 1.0 L***

1339 1.5 L***

1340 0.5 L***

1342 1.5 L

1343 0.5 L***

1344 0.5 L***

MOLD	SIZE	STYLE	SCENE
1334	0.5 L	ETCHED	Gasthaus scene, two seated men, standing woman, ***
1335	0.5 L	ETCHED	Woman playing piano, ***
1336	1.0 L	ETCHED	Sitting man teasing seated barmaid, ***
1337	0.5 L	ETCHED	*Kaiser Karl der Grosse*, ***
1338	1.0 L	ETCHED	Tavern scene with man courting maid, ***
1339	1.5 L	ETCHED	Tavern scene with dog on table on a stein, ***
1340	0.5 L	ETCHED	Heidelberg scene, ***
1342	1.5 L	RELIEF	Seated couple in forest, she is sewing, he is dreaming
1343	0.5 L	ETCHED AND RELIEF	Two men, one woman with table, ***
1344	0.5 L	ETCHED AND RELIEF	Three Bavarian boys at table with dancing couple, ***

| 1346 0.5 L*** | 1347 0.5 L*** | 1348 0.5 L*** | 1349 1.0 L*** | 1349 0.5 L |

| 1351 1.0 L*** | 1352 1.5 L*** | 1353 1.0 L*** | 1354 1.0 L*** | 1356 0.5 L*** |

MOLD	SIZE	STYLE	SCENE
1346	0.5 L	ETCHED AND RELIEF	Cavalier and maiden sitting on a bench, ***
1347	0.5 L	ETCHED AND RELIEF	Woman playing trumpet with cavalier behind, ***
1348	0.5 L	ETCHED AND RELIEF	Zither player and standing woman, ***
1349	1.0 L	ETCHED AND RELIEF	Maid serving seated man with dog in chair, ***
1349	0.5 L	RELIEF	Dancing cavaliers, vine style
1351	1.0 L	ETCHED AND RELIEF	Tavern, seated man with barmaid, man at table, ***
1352	1.5 L	ETCHED AND RELIEF	Barmaid dancing for men in tavern, ***
1353	1.0 L	ETCHED AND RELIEF	*Neckerei*, teasing, soldier and woman sitting on bench, ***
1354	1.0 L	ETCHED AND RELIEF	Deck scene, two seated men, a woman, and girl, ***
1356	0.5 L	ETCHED AND RELIEF	Three men leaving maid plus a child with a backpack, ***

1358 0.5 L***   1359 2.5 L***   1360 2.0 L***   1361 3.0 L***   1369 0.25 L***

1369 0.25 L***   1370 0.3 L***   1375 2.0 L***   1378 0.5 L***   1381 0.5 L

MOLD	SIZE	STYLE	SCENE
1358	0.5 L	ETCHED AND RELIEF	Gasthaus scene, *Speckbacher und sohn anderle*, ***
1359	2.5 L	ETCHED	Girl with military hat saluting table of men, ***
1360	2.0 L	ETCHED	Tavern scene, with drunk *landsknecht* on floor, ***
1361	3.0 L	ETCHED	The shooting king showing off his award, ***
1369	0.25 L	ETCHED	Man pumping wine into barrel, ***
1369	0.25 L	ETCHED	Man pumping wine into barrel, salt glaze fired, ***
1370	0.3 L	ETCHED	Cherub handing wine to musician, ***
1375	2.0 L	ETCHED	*Kaiser Karl der Grosse*, ***
1378	0.5 L	ETCHED	Bowling scene, base of moons on green field, ***
1381	0.5 L	RELIEF	Renaissance dancing couple

1385 0.4 L***

1386 0.3 L***

1387 0.25 L***

1388 1.5 L***

1390 3.0 L***

1393 0.5 L***

1394 0.5 L***

1395 0.5 L***

1396 0.5 L***

1397 1.5 L***

MOLD	SIZE	STYLE	SCENE
1385	0.4 L	ETCHED AND RELIEF	Two standing cavaliers, plus saying, ***
1386	0.3 L	ETCHED AND RELIEF	Hunter hugging maiden, outdoor scene, ***
1387	0.25 L	ETCHED AND RELIEF	Man with guitar serenading lady, in gasthaus, ***
1388	1.5 L	RELIEF	*Eine Scharfe Partie*, card game, similar to 1397, ***
1390	3.0 L	ETCHED	Seated hunter or hiker with maid, drinking a glass, ***
1393	0.5 L	ETCHED	Junior, ***
1394	0.5 L	ETCHED	Freshy, ***
1395	0.5 L	ETCHED	Soph, ***
1396	0.5 L	ETCHED	Senior, ***
1397	1.5 L	ETCHED	*Eine Scharfe Partie*, card game, similar to 1388, ***

1398 2.0 L***

1409 0.5 L***

1410 0.5 L***

1411 1.0 L*

1412 0.3 L*

1413 1.0 L*

1414 0.5 L***

1420 1.5 L

1429 0.3 L***

1430 0.4 L***

MOLD	SIZE	STYLE	SCENE
1398	2.0 L	ETCHED	Tavern scene of several men focused on maid, all seated, ***
1409	0.5 L	ETCHED	Dianna the hunter, ***
1410	0.5 L	ETCHED	Outdoor bowling scene, ***
1411	1.0 L	ETCHED	Gasthaus scene, relief elk above scene, *
1412	0.3 L	ETCHED	Gasthaus scene, two men, waitress, and mandolin player, *
1413	1.0 L	ETCHED	Couple showing puppies to hunter, *
1414	0.5 L	CHARACTER	*Frauenkirche* tower, Munich Child, ***
1420	1.5 L	RELIEF	Man and woman in keller toasting each other with wine
1429	0.3 L	ETCHED	Handled beaker, walking couple, ***
1430	0.4 L	ETCHED	*Schloss Heidelberg*, ***

1431 0.4 L***

1433 2.0 L***

1434 0.3 L*

1452 0.5 L***

1453 0.5 L***

1461 1.0 L

1466 0.25 L*

1466 1.0 L

1467 1.0 L

1470 0.25 L***

MOLD	SIZE	STYLE	SCENE
1431	0.4 L	ETCHED	Kaiser Wilhelm Memorial, ***
1433	2.0 L	ETCHED	Tavern hunting scene, high-glaze accents, ***
1434	0.3 L	ETCHED	Fancy glaze, tavern, *Beim Fruhschoppen*, *
1452	0.5 L	ETCHED	4F, two muscular men with banner and barrel, ***
1453	0.5 L	ETCHED	Bicyclist with flag, ***
1461	1.0 L	RELIEF	Three hikers, outdoor scene, motto in English, post-WWII
1466	0.25 L	RELIEF	Munich scenes, *
1466	1.0 L	RELIEF	Standing man and seated woman, three dogs, post-WWII
1467	1.0 L	RELIEF	Card players, post-WWII
1470	0.25 L	ETCHED	Boy and girl dancing with boy playing flute, ***

1473 0.5 L*

1474 0.5 L*

1475 0.5 L*

1485 0.5 L***

1490 0.5 L***

1492 0.5 L***

1493 0.5 L***

1495 0.5 L***

1496 1.0 L*

1497 2.0 L*

MOLD	SIZE	STYLE	SCENE
1473	0.5 L	ETCHED	Three cavaliers playing whist or *skat*, *
1474	0.5 L	ETCHED	Three men courting woman seated around barrel, *
1475	0.5 L	ETCHED	Cavalier playing mandolin, *
1485	0.5 L	ETCHED	Tavern scene, three seated men focused on maiden, ***
1490	0.5 L	ETCHED	Knight and maiden riding horses, ***
1492	0.5 L	ETCHED	Outdoor gasthaus scene, three men, two women, ***
1493	0.5 L	ETCHED	Woman playing guitar for three men drinking wine, ***
1495	0.5 L	ETCHED	Cavalier and lady at base of stairs, ***
1496	1.0 L	ETCHED	Gladiator and bull scene, *
1497	2.0 L	ETCHED	*Falstaff's Rekruten Musterung*, court scene, *

1498 1.5 L*	1499 1.0 L***	1512 0.125 L	1579 0.5 L***	1632 1.0 L

1637 0.5 L*	1648 0.25 L	1696 0.25 L	1729 0.5 L	1864 0.5 L

MOLD	SIZE	STYLE	SCENE
1498	1.5 L	ETCHED	Woman with huge master stein pouring for youth, *
1499	1.0 L	ETCHED	Boy carrying sword and shield, fat man, and clerk, ***
1512	0.125 L	RELIEF	Boy with mandolin playing for girl across fence, post-WWII
1579	0.5 L	ETCHED	*Waidmanns Heil*, outdoor hunting scene, ***
1632	1.0 L	RELIEF	Outdoor scene, card players with monk, post-WWII
1637	0.5 L	RELIEF	Jugendstil birds on flowers, unusual bright-orange color, *
1648	0.25 L	RELIEF	Zither player with girl, post-WWII
1696	0.25 L	RELIEF	Hunter sitting with dog, pheasant, and rifle, post-WWII
1729	0.5 L	RELIEF	Tavern scene, hunter, barmaid, guitarist, post-WWII
1864	0.5 L	RELIEF	Mihan design, University of Portland, dated 1952

11013 0.3 L

11014 0.25 L

11020 1.0 L

11022 1.5 L

11024 2.0 L

11026 0.75 L

11029 1.0 L

11034 0.5 L

11035 0.5 L

11038 0.5 L

MOLD	SIZE	STYLE	SCENE
11013	0.3 L	ETCHED	Man and maiden dancing outdoors (1013)
11014	0.25 L	ETCHED	Keller scene (1014)
11020	1.0 L	RELIEF	Five standing musicians and singers, 1500s dress (1020)
11022	1.5 L	RELIEF	Outdoor barbarians gathering (1022)
11024	2.0 L	RELIEF	Outdoor gasthaus scene (1024)
11026	0.75 L	RELIEF	Flute player with three others at table, *Ein Flotensolo* (1026)
11029	1.0 L	RELIEF	Gasthaus scene, musician, two women, three men (1029)
11034	0.5 L	ETCHED	Jugendstil, artistic bands top and bottom (1034)
11035	0.5 L	RELIEF	Outdoor drinkers almost fighting (1035)
11038	0.5 L	RELIEF	*Schuhplattler*, dancer (1038)

11040 0.5 L

11041 0.5 L

11042 1.0 L

11042 1.0 L

11044 1.0 L

11045 1.0 L *

11045 1.0 L

11049 1.0 L

11058 0.5 L

11058 0.5 L

MOLD	SIZE	STYLE	SCENE
11040	0.5 L	RELIEF	Deer or *Hirsch* (1040)
11041	0.5 L	ETCHED	Deer in field, hunting scene (1041)
11042	1.0 L	RELIEF	Outdoor scene, two musicians and four dancers (1042)
11042	1.0 L	RELIEF	Two musicians, four dancers outdoors, recessed base (1042)
11044	1.0 L	RELIEF	Three renaissance men, woman, and mandolin player (1044)
11045	1.0 L	RELIEF	Norse scene, horse, harp, several soldiers, * (1045)
11045	1.0 L	RELIEF	Same scene as above, recessed base (1045)
11049	1.0 L	RELIEF	*Lustige Gesellschaft* (1049)
11058	0.5 L	CHARACTER	Barrel, *Wohl bekomm's!* (1058)
11058	0.5 L	CHARACTER	Barrel, salt glaze with custom name "Willy Urban" (1058)

11065 1.5 L

11066 3.0 L

11067 2.0 L

11068 1.5 L

11070 1.0 L

11071 1.0 L

11072 1.0 L

11074 0.5 L

11088 1.0 L

11089 1.0 L

MOLD	SIZE	STYLE	SCENE
11065	1.5 L	RELIEF	Renaissance man, two women on horse plus dogs (1065)
11066	3.0 L	RELIEF	Old German outdoor scene (1066)
11067	2.0 L	ETCHED	Cavaliers, high-glaze relief bands (1067)
11068	1.5 L	ETCHED	Couple in renaissance dress (1068)
11070	1.0 L	ETCHED	Wedding with knights, Gambrinus figural (1070)
11071	1.0 L	RELIEF	Dancing couple in 1700s dress, two seated musicians (1071)
11072	1.0 L	ETCHED	Dutch scene (1072)
11074	0.5 L	RELIEF	Tavern scene, violinist playing to group (1074)
11088	1.0 L	RELIEF	Group carrying food trays, with musicians (1088)
11089	1.0 L	RELIEF	Renaissance scene, solitary woman and five men (1089)

| 11090 1.0 L | 11091 2.0 L | 11092 2.5 L | 11094 1.5 L | 11095 2.0 L |

| 11098 1.0 L | 11102 0.5 L | 11103 0.5 L | 11104 0.5 L | 11106 0.5 L |

MOLD	SIZE	STYLE	SCENE
11090	1.0 L	RELIEF	Renaissance troubadours (1090)
11091	2.0 L	RELIEF	Cavalier on horseback with attendants (1091)
11092	2.5 L	RELIEF	Medieval king on horse with waiters in courtyard (1092)
11094	1.5 L	ETCHED	Dutch women in the country (1094)
11095	2.0 L	ETCHED	Dutch countryside, courting couple (1095)
11098	1.0 L	ETCHED	Dutch scene, boy and girl in the countryside (1098)
11102	0.5 L	RELIEF	Four cavaliers sitting around barrel drinking, vine style (1102)
11103	0.5 L	RELIEF	Three cavaliers and woman sitting around a barrel (1103)
11104	0.5 L	RELIEF	Chess match (1104)
11106	0.5 L	RELIEF	Two knights on horseback following a walking couple (1106)

11108 0.5 L

11111 0.75 L

11114 1.5 L

11115 1.0 L

11117 1.0 L

11118 1.0 L

11119 1.0 L

11121 1.5 L

11127 2.0 L

11128 2.0 L

MOLD	SIZE	STYLE	SCENE
11108	0.5 L	RELIEF	BPOE elk, two hunters, and motto (modified from 1108)
11111	0.75 L	RELIEF	Germans introducing beer to Roman soldiers (1111)
11114	1.5 L	RELIEF	Late 1700s dance and toast (1114)
11115	1.0 L	RELIEF	Group pulling beer wagon by hand (1115)
11117	1.0 L	RELIEF	Two couples and three women, outdoor scene (1117)
11118	1.0 L	RELIEF	Two couples dancing, old men seated, drinking (1118)
11119	1.0 L	RELIEF	*Fingerhakeln*, finger-twisting game (1119)
11121	1.5 L	RELIEF	Man and woman,1700s dress, with several watchers (1121)
11127	2.0 L	RELIEF	BPOE elk, two hunters (modified from 1127)
11128	2.0 L	RELIEF	Several women outdoors with radishes and fruit (1128)

Permission of Les Paul

11129 1.5 L   11130 2.0 L   11131 2.0 L   11132 0.5 L   11146 1.0 L

11147 2.0 L   11149 0.5 L   11150 0.5 L   11154 0.4 L   11165 1.5 L

MOLD	SIZE	STYLE	SCENE
11129	1.5 L	RELIEF	1700s drinking scene, fortune-teller (1129)
11130	2.0 L	RELIEF	Drinking horn, historismus design (1130)
11131	2.0 L	CHARACTER	Bowling Pin (1131)
11132	0.5 L	CHARACTER	Bowling Pin (1132)
11146	1.0 L	RELIEF	Men bowling with strike, couple drinking plus dog (1146)
11147	2.0 L	RELIEF	Soldiers taking man with fan collar (1147)
11149	0.5 L	RELIEF	Night watchman, mandolin player, woman, man (1149)
11150	0.5 L	RELIEF	Three renaissance men, mandolin player with mugs (1150)
11154	0.4 L	RELIEF	Three men, stein, pitcher, pipe, barrel, and dog (1154)
11165	1.5 L	RELIEF	Man running, soldier and girl dancing (1165)

11166 2.0 L   11167 3.0 L   11176 0.5 L   11180 0.5 L   11181 0.5 L

11182 0.5 L   11185 0.5 L   11187 0.5 L   11189 1.5 L   11195 1.0 L

MOLD	SIZE	STYLE	SCENE
11166	2.0 L	RELIEF	Entertainers, dancer and clown (1166)
11167	3.0 L	RELIEF	Woman on horse almost kissing knight, heavy relief (1167)
11176	0.5 L	RELIEF	Student frogs drinking (1176)
11180	0.5 L	ETCHED	Freemasons (1180)
11181	0.5 L	ETCHED	Common phrase, 1920s (1181)
11182	0.5 L	RELIEF	Sleeping man with barrel and bottles, English text (1182)
11185	0.5 L	RELIEF	Several deer in forest, rabbit handle (1185)
11187	0.5 L	RELIEF	Gasthaus scene, with mandolin player (1187)
11189	1.5 L	RELIEF	Barbarian leading horse to horn-blower beside deer (1189)
11195	1.0 L	RELIEF	Student frog scene, *Auf die Mensur*, (1195)

11196 1.0 L   11201 3.0 L   11205 0.5 L   11206 0.5 L   11215 1.5 L

11226 2.5 L   11227 2.0 L   11228 2.0 L   11238 0.5 L   11245 1.0 L

MOLD	SIZE	STYLE	SCENE
11196	1.0 L	RELIEF	Old German, monk, Gambrinus, modern man (1196)
11201	3.0 L	RELIEF	Hunters and deer, with fox handle (1201)
11205	0.5 L	RELIEF	Dogs chasing stag, rabbit figural lid, fox handle (1205)
11206	0.5 L	RELIEF	Hunting scene in forest with deer, dogs, and hunters (1206)
11215	1.5 L	RELIEF	Two men in Viking boat in storm, art deco, green glaze
11226	2.5 L	RELIEF	A gathering around a barrel, two women, three men (1226)
11227	2.0 L	RELIEF	Stag with several doe in background (1227)
11228	2.0 L	RELIEF	Stag and deer (1228)
11238	0.5 L	RELIEF	Same stag as 11228 (1238)
11245	1.0 L	RELIEF	Fox hunting scene (1245)

| 11247 0.75 L | 11248 0.5 L | 11249 0.5 L | 11254 0.3 L | 11257 0.5 L |

| 11297 1.0 L | 11299 0.5 L | 11308 0.5 L | XXX8 0.5 L | XXX2 0.5 L |

MOLD	SIZE	STYLE	SCENE
11247	0.75 L	RELIEF	Grist mill with dancers and bagpipes, LDB & C logo (1247)
11248	0.5 L	RELIEF	Stag foreground plus five deer in background (1248)
11249	0.5 L	RELIEF	Soccer match (1249)
11254	0.3 L	RELIEF	Waitress pouring glass for seated man, dancer (1254)
11257	0.5 L	RELIEF	Battleships, sailor handle, *Trinkt Bruder*..., (1257)
11297	1.0 L	CHARACTER	Tower, watchman, drunks, owl, verse, sun, moon (1297)
11299	0.5 L	CHARACTER	Tower with clock faces, cat handle (1299)
11308	0.5 L	RELIEF	Gnome king surrounded by fellow gnomes (1308)
XXX8	0.5 L	RELIEF	Passed out drunk surrounded by barrels, English text
XXX2	0.5 L	ETCHED	Man holding two barrels and sitting on one, English text

1.5 L	1.0 L	0.5 L	0.4 L	1.0 L

2.0 L	0.5 L	2.0 Kg	1.0 Kg	1170 0.5 L

MOLD	SIZE	STYLE	SCENE
none	1.5 L	Reetemacht incised	Oval logo, August Remy's designs from 1920s
none	1.0 L	Reetemacht incised	Logo free-standing, August Remy's designs from 1920s
none	0.5 L	Reetemacht incised	Oval logo, August Remy's designs from 1920s
none	0.4 L	Reetemacht incised	Logo free-standing, August Remy's designs from 1920s
none	1.0 L	RELIEF	Alpen Queen, no logo
none	2.0 L	Reetemacht incised	Milk jug, flowers, and bars, scratched design, hand-thrown
none	0.5 L	RELIEF	Jugendstil, circles and verticals, unusual from J. W. Remy
none	2.0 Kg	RELIEF	Tobacco jar, *Kautabak von Grimm und Triepel in Nordhausen*
none	1.0 Kg	RELIEF	Tobacco jar, *Kneiff Kautabak*, *Nordhausen*
1170	0.5 L	RELIEF	Tower, cavalier with guitar serenading young woman, no logo

0.125 L*	0.125 L*	0.5 L*	0.125 L*	0.25 L*

0.5 L	0.25 L	0.5 L	0.5 L	0.5 L

MOLD	SIZE	STYLE	SCENE
none	0.125 L	RELIEF	*Ashenbroedel*, Cinderella scene, *
none	0.125 L	RELIEF	Souvenir of Philadelphia, Independence Hall, *
none	0.5 L	PRINT OVER GLAZE	Gasthaus, seated man with two women, one holding tuba, *
none	0.125 L	RELIEF	Boy and girl with spinning wheel, *
none	0.25 L	RELIEF	Part of set 1058 and 1066, *
none	0.5 L	RELIEF	MA Institute of Technology, seal, two seated students
none	0.25 L	RELIEF	Lewis and Clark Exposition, Portland, Oregon
none	0.5 L	RELIEF	Lewis and Clark Exposition, Portland, Oregon
none	0.5 L	ETCHED	The US Capitol, Washington, DC, no logo
none	0.5 L	ETCHED	Library of Congress, Washington, DC, no logo

0.5 L

0.5 L

0.5 L

0.5 L

0.5 L

0.25 L

0.25 L

0.25 L

0.125 L

0.25 L

MOLD	SIZE	STYLE	SCENE
None	0.5 L	RELIEF	Soldiers monument, Indianapolis (handle identification)
None	0.5 L	RELIEF	City hall, Milwaukee (handle identification)
None	0.5 L	RELIEF	Courthouse, Davenport (handle identification)
None	0.5 L	RELIEF	Union Station, St. Louis (handle identification)
None	0.5 L	RELIEF	State capitol, Albany (handle identification)
None	0.25 L	RELIEF	City hall, Milwaukee (handle identification)
None	0.25 L	RELIEF	Milwaukee, souvenir (handle identification)
None	0.25 L	RELIEF	Cornell University (handle identification)
None	0.125 L	RELIEF	Little Red Riding Hood (handle identification)
None	0.25 L	RELIEF	Puzzle jug (dancers same as 314 and 349)

AFTERWORD

When I decided to write this book, I had little idea where my research would lead. As my work progressed, I came to realize that when personal relationships are interwoven with business, the activities, motivations, and decisions that might normally be documented as part of a business history can be lost, or at least obscured. The records of the two companies—J. W. Remy and J. P. Thewalt—are nowhere near as complete as I had hoped, and the intervening decades have forced a certain amount of supposition and speculation in my study of these two companies.

I have spent more than twenty-five years collecting information on both the J. W. Remy and J. P. Thewalt companies and have devoted nearly ten years working on this book. Throughout the process, I have gained more insight into the complications of each company and their familial relationship.

My hope is that after perusing this book about J. W. Remy, you will have a greater appreciation, not only for the company itself, but also for the German history that is expressed in J. W. Remy steins.

APPENDIX 1

The Relationship between J. W. Remy
and J. P. Thewalt

Historical Review

The firm of J. P. Thewalt was founded in 1852, and that of J. W. Remy in 1860. Karl Thewalt, the son of Johann Peter Thewalt, Jr., assumed operating control of J. P. Thewalt following his father's death in 1887. The following year, J. W.'s daughter Anna Remy married Karl. Many towns of the region and time were little larger than small villages, and intermarriage between families of competing potteries was common.

It has been well documented that J. W. Remy's production growth was limited. J. W. Remy apparently had the funds to build a much-needed additional firing kiln, but the factory's location in the center of Höhr prevented expansion.

A solution was created by establishing a business relationship with son-in-law Karl Thewalt around 1890. Since the two factories were located within walking distance of each other, J. W. Remy built a kiln on the J. P. Thewalt factory property. Both companies benefited from the increased firing capacity and apparently merged several other factory operations, likely about the same time. The two companies continued their relationship until after Karl's death in 1923.

Albert J. Thewalt III (great-grandson of J. P. Thewalt, Jr.) suggested that 150 years ago, family, in German society, was often more important than business issues. As a result of that marriage, we have to interpret the history of these firms and families as one family, two businesses.

This characteristic of German life of the period helps explain the similarities between the two companies' steins. There are two important customs of the time to remember. First, it was common for family members to work together sharing the production work. At the same time, company sales and marketing information were kept separate. These factors explain both the similarities of their steins as well as the overlapping model numbering systems.

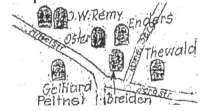

Höhr map of relative locations of
J. W. Remy and J. P. Thewalt kilns

| JWR 882 | JPT 1473 | JWR 855 | JPT 1475 |

Examples of inlays from J. W. Remy and J. P. Thewalt steins that have logo identifications

Shared Production Responsibilities

There are no records to tell us how the J. W. Remy and J. P. Thewalt firms shared production responsibilities beyond sharing the kiln. It seems apparent that they merged some processes for efficiency and cost savings. One such example was in the development of new designs. J. W.'s son August was the chief modeler for J. W. Remy. It is probable that he oversaw many of J. P. Thewalt's designs and modeling as well. In fact, Roland Henschen stated in his *Prosit* article in December 1985 that J. W. Remy shared technology with J. P. Thewalt in addition to selling molds to them. By analyzing the artwork of each company's wares, evidence strongly indicates that many were modeled by the same designer.

There are a number of additional similarities in the output from each firm. Colors and finish textures are similar, indicating the use of the same clays, glazes, and firing temperatures (which would be expected, since they used the same kiln). Capacity marks and logo fonts are similar. They may have used the same metal stamp supplier or utilized a shared production line, or both. There are many identical inlays found on each other's steins; inlay designs must have been shared. The same is true for many handle designs.

Each company kept its own distinct molds separate (even if the molds had been provided by one company). Combining purchases of glaze supplies to save money would explain the similarity of glaze types and colors. The similarity of inlays, handles, and modeling styles (such as beaded bands) suggests a more intertwined relationship, but records available today do not provide details.

Attribution of Steins without Company Logos

Few pieces by either J. W. Remy or J. P. Thewalt bear logos, and without referring to the J. W. Remy Model Book and available JWR and JPT catalogs, it is very easy to mistake the work of one firm for that of the other. The first discriminant is the model number, which, thankfully, is present on almost all wares produced by both companies.

The above-mentioned reference documents indicate that J. W. Remy used model numbers ranging from 50 to 1950. While the sole J. P. Thewalt catalog is limited to *relief* models in the range of 1000 to 1200, known examples of *etched* steins bearing the *JPT* logo extend that range as high as 1637. There is no evidence that J. W. Remy produced *etched* steins in that range. Both companies' catalogs and the Model Book provide the means to identify the producer of *relief* steins in the range from 1000 to 1200.

- *Etched* and *relief* steins with model numbers between 50 and 1000 were made by JWR.

- *Etched* steins with model numbers between 1000 and 1200 were made by JWR.

- *Relief* steins with model numbers between 1000 and 1200 can usually be identified by referring to available catalogs or the J. W. Remy Model Book.

- Steins with model numbers between 1637 and 1950 were made by JWR.

- Etched steins with model numbers between 1200 and 1637 carrying *JPT* logos were likely made by JPT.

This would seem to wrap up the attribution question, if it weren't for the pesky five-digit model numbers mentioned in chapter 3, sixty-four of which are shown in the pictorial catalog. In this group, only two pieces bear a company logo—one *JWR*, one *JPT*. However, in every case, when the leading *1* is eliminated, the stein can be matched to a stein in the J. W. Remy Model Book or catalogs. As hypothesized earlier, the apparent reason for this was to avoid conflict with JPT steins bearing the same four-digit model numbers. Since the molds of these steins were originally part of J. W. Remy's production, it is likely that the steins were all produced by Remy, and the single JPT-marked example is a mistaken marking as steins were prepared for firing. Based on this reasoning, steins with five-digit model numbers were likely made by J.W Remy.

Wrap-Up

Many of the beer steins previously attributed to J. W. Remy were probably supplied by J. P. Thewalt. Is this significant? What if, for example, J. W. Remy was unable to meet the demand for its steins? A solution might have been to seek help from a closely related family pottery (that is, J. P. Thewalt). This would allow both companies to expand their businesses, and it might be an important reason why original designs made by J. W. Remy were provided to J. P. Thewalt. It should be noted, on the other hand, that all J. W. Remy steins are identified in specific ways. They have a logo, are pictured in catalogs, or are described in the Model Book.

All J. W. Remy designs are distinctly different from those with the same model numbers marked with the JPT logo or those pictured in the J. P. Thewalt catalog. The same is true for its etched steins.

Historically, unmarked etched steins have been attributed to J. W. Remy due to the similarities. With these new insights, it is now known that both companies were involved in manufacturing these steins. That assumption is supported by the significant quantity of JPT-marked etched steins.

There remain many unanswered questions regarding the relationship between J. W. Remy and J. P. Thewalt. However, there is better understanding of the reasons for the similarities of each other's steins in color, style, and design.

J. W. REMY

Mold	Image	Page	Size	Finish	Description
1013	CATALOG	9A	0.5 L	ETCHED	Dancers
1014	BOOK		0.25 L	ETCHED	In the keller
1015	BOOK		0.3 L	RELIEF	Drink with friend
1016	CATALOG	5A	0.5 L	ETCHED	Jugendstil
1017	CATALOG	5A	0.5 L	ETCHED	Jugendstil
1018	BOOK		0.4 L	RELIEF	Picture
1019	BOOK		0.4 L	RELIEF	Hunter
1020	BOOK		1.5 L	ETCHED	Image
1021	BOOK		2.0 L	RELIEF	Bringing beer
1022	BOOK		1.5 L	RELIEF	*...bei Koenig reug?*
1023	CATALOG	6A	2.5 L	RELIEF	Barbarians
1024	CATALOG	6A	2.0 L	RELIEF	Gasthaus scene
1025	BOOK		0.5 L	RELIEF	Picture saying
1026	BOOK		0.75 L	RELIEF	*Ein Flutensolo*
1027	BOOK		1.0 L	RELIEF	Knight
1291	BOOK		0.25 L	RELIEF	Indecipherable
1292	BOOK		0.25 L	RELIEF	Indecipherable
1293	BOOK		1.0 L	RELIEF	Similar to 1282
1294	BOOK		1.5 L	RELIEF	Similar to 1282
1295	BOOK		0.75 L	RELIEF	Similar to 1282
1296	BOOK		1.25 L	UNKNOWN	Forest party
1297	BOOK		0.75 L	RELIEF	Horn inlay

J. P. THEWALT

Image	Page	Size	Finish	Description
CATALOG	1	0.5 L	RELIEF	Cartouche
CATALOG	1	0.5 L	RELIEF	Woman front
CATALOG	3	0.5 L	RELIEF	Outdoors
EMPTY				
EMPTY				
CATALOG	2	0.5 L	RELIEF	Cartouche couple
CATALOG	2	0.5 L	RELIEF	Maid at table
CATALOG	3	0.5 L	RELIEF	Maid on fence
CATALOG	3	0.5 L	RELIEF	Courting couple
CATALOG	3	0.5 L	RELIEF	Seated man & dog
CATALOG	3	0.5 L	RELIEF	Maid and two men
CATALOG	3	0.5 L	RELIEF	Couple and barrel
CATALOG	1	0.5 L	RELIEF	Tavern scene
CATALOG	1	0.5 L	RELIEF	Three cartouches
PHOTO		1.5 L	RELIEF	Card game
CATALOG MKD		0.5 L	ETCHED	Couple, mandolin
PHOTO		0.5 L	ETCHED	Keller courting
CATALOG MKD		0.25 L	ETCHED	Couple talking
CATALOG MKD		0.4 L	ETCHED	Tavern couple
PHOTO		0.3 L	ETCHED	Glutton in keller
CATALOG MKD		1.0 L	ETCHED	Cavalier party
PHOTO		0.4 L	ETCHED	Musician, maids

A comparison of spreadsheet entries of both J. W. Remy and J. P. Thewalt steins.
Taken from catalogs, the Model Book, and marked (MKD) examples.

APPENDIX 2

A Brief Overview of the J. P. Thewalt Firm

The J. P. Thewalt firm was founded in 1852 by Johann Peter (J. P.) Thewalt, Jr. The firm was located at Bergstrasse 1a in the village of Höhr. In 1887, J. P. passed on, and in the tradition of the period, his eldest son, Karl, inherited the factory. A huge benefit of Karl's marriage to Anna Remy was the joining of both J. P. Thewalt and J. W. Remy firms. Being almost a block apart enabled the two companies to combine their wares in the same kiln.

Karl Thewalt managed the company until his death ca. 1923. His son Hubert continued the operation until its closure ca. 1930.

The close relationship between the firms of J. P. Thewalt and J. W. Remy ended shortly after Karl Thewalt's death in 1923. Management of the J. P. Thewalt company at the time was assumed by Karl and Anna's son Hubert Thewalt. Both principals of the original alliance had passed on, and the remaining management apparently had different plans regarding the future of the relationship. Hubert continued to operate the J. P. Thewalt company until it was shut down around 1930.

The closure was indicative of the time. Germany's period of severe depression and uncontrolled inflation following the First World War caused severe financial hardship for nearly every company. Many businesses of the time likewise failed.

Karl's widow, Anna Remy Thewalt, oversaw the closure as the chief officer of the J. P. Thewalt company. The assets, including buildings and property, were taken over by the stoneware firm of Eckhardt and Engler. According to Roland Henschen, all J. P. Thewalt molds were destroyed at that time.

After the business was dissolved, Anna moved back to her childhood home at Mittelstrasse 7 and lived out her remaining years.

Ron Gray provided an interesting footnote about J. P. Thewalt in his December 2010 *Prosit* article. He wrote that in 1882, J. P. Thewalt, Jr.'s younger son Albert J. Thewalt decided to strike out on his own. He founded Paulus & Thewalt GmbH with a brother-in-law. The firm, which is still in business today, manufactured ceramic products for the pharmaceutical industry. A few years later, he left that company to start his own business, which was associated with cork materials around the 1890s. He then started a pottery and hired modeler Wilhelm Kamp to design a line of beer steins for his new company, A. J. Thewalt.

The decision by Albert to directly compete with his brother Karl caused a major rift within the family. For many years, there was limited communication between the two companies.

SOURCES

I have relied on many sources to write this book, and I am grateful for all, even if not mentioned, for the ideas, suggestions, and encouragement.

Articles

Baaden, Franz. *"Das Kannenbäckerland und seine Ausstrahlungen." Die Schaulade*, May 1981.

Gray, Ron. "Albert Jacob Thewalt GmbH." *Prosit*, September 2010.

Gray, Ron. "Albert Jacob Thewalt GmbH." *Prosit*, December 2010.

Henschen, Roland. "The Thewalt 'TP' Mark." From the Stein Makers series. *Prosit*, December 1985.

Joshpe, Glen. "In Search of J. W. Remy—Part II." *Prosit*, March 1983.

Joshpe, Glen. "In Search of J. W. Remy—Part III." *Prosit*, December 1985.

Books

Fries, Heribert. *Alt Hoehr-Grenzhausen*. Höhr-Grenzhausen: self-published, 1986.

Kessler, Gerd. *Meine Erinnerungen an die Firma J. W. Remy*. Höhr-Grenzhausen: self-published, 2000.

Mayen, Klaus-Dieter. *Tongraeber im Westerwald*. Germany: Unknown publisher, 1985.

Mueller, Ilse, et. al. *Die Familie Remy, Kannenbacker und Unternehmer, Eine genealogische Bestandsaufnahme*. Tubingen: LEGAT Verlag GmbH & Co., 2009.

Hammond Incorporated. *Hammond World Atlas, Gemini Edition*. Maplewood, New Jersey: Hammond World Atlas Corp, 1991.

Sitwell, N.H.H. *Roman Roads of Europe*. New York: St. Martin's Press, 1981.

Zezschwitz, Beate Dry-v. *Historismus, Angewandte Kunst im 19. Jahrhundert, Band 2: Kunsthandwerk und Kunstgewerbe*. Kassel: Staatliche Museen, 1989.

Zezschwitz, Beate Dry-v. *R. Merkelbach, Grenzhausen und Muenchen.* Muenchen: Verlag Dr. Graham Dry, 1981.

Zezschwitz, Beate Dry-v. *Westerwälder Steinzeug des Jugendstils 1900–1914: Stilstufen in der Entwicklung einer neuen Steinzeugkunst.* Muenchen: Ludwig-Maximilians-Universität, 1993.

Maps

Bürgermeister, Mrs. Hedwig Carola (dec.). Maps of Höhr and Grenzhausen salt-glaze kilns, pre-1930.

Thewalt III, Albert J. City of Höhr factories.

Personal Communications

Kessler, Gerd, great-grandson of J. W. Remy. Discussions.

Thewalt III, Albert J., great-grandson of J. P. Thewalt. Discussions.

Presentations

Ammelounx, Andre. "Eric P. Mihan." Details of J. W. Remy's participation in Mihan's college stein program. Copy of the artwork for the University of Portland, Oregon, stein. Presented at Stein Collectors International Convention, San Francisco, California, September 25, 2009.

Kessler, Gerd. "Stoneware History from the Westerwald." Presented at the Ceramics Symposium at Colonial Williamsburg, Williamsburg, Virginia, March 18, 2010.

Websites

Harr, David. "J. W. Remy Character Steins." www.charactersteins.com/cs-book/JW.Remy.htm. Site discontinued.

Loevi, Frank. "J. P. Thewalt Stein Catalog." The Beer Stein Library. https://www.beerstein.net/catalog.asp?id=36. Accessed March, 2020.

Loevi, Frank. "J. W. Remy Stein Catalog." The Beer Stein Library. https://www.beerstein.net/catalog.asp?id=29. Accessed November 2019.

Stein Collectors International. www.stein-collectors.org. Accessed ongoing since 2002.

Wheeler, Chris. "Home." Stein Marks. http://www.steinmarks.co.uk. Accessed ongoing since March 2010.

Wheeler, Chris. "Stein Marks." Stein Marks. http://www.steinmarks.co.uk/pages/pv.asp?p=stein203. Accessed March 2010.

ABOUT THE AUTHOR

This is Lyn Ayers' first foray into researching and writing a full-length book, although writing is not a new activity. He has published many articles in the Stein Collectors International (SCI) quarterly newsletter *Prosit*. He is well known in the stein-collecting community for his research and commitment to the hobby and has been a featured speaker about J. W. Remy at several SCI conventions. SCI recognized Lyn for his original research by presenting him with the prestigious Master Steinologist Award in 2007. He served the organization for seventeen years as the librarian/museum director. In researching this book, he traveled to Germany on several occasions.

Outside of beer steins, Lyn had a productive career in technical electronics sales. He also served as president of Clark County Rental Association for more than ten years.

He currently lives in Washington State in the house he and his wife, Janine, purchased in 1974, which was followed by nearly seven years of extensive remodeling and updating. They presently share that home with two indoor rescue cats.

CPSIA information can be obtained
at www.ICGtesting.com
Printed in the USA
LVHW071820280622
722288LV00011B/168